# APPROACHES IN CRIMINAL PROFILING

AN INTRODUCTION

DAVID ELIO MALOCCO

B.C.L., B.Sc. (Psych), Dip. F.Sc., Dip. P.C.P.

ISBN: 1507802129
ISBN-13: 978-1507802120

# DEDICATION

To Colette.

# CONTENTS

# ACKNOWLEDGMENTS

Thanks to Gary Power for his work on the cover and interior.

# 1 INTRODUCTION

*In solving a problem of this sort, the grand thing is to be able to reason backward. That is a very useful accomplishment, and a very easy one, but people do not practise it much. In the everyday affairs of life it is more useful to reason forward, and so the other comes to be neglected. There are fifty who can reason synthetically for one who can reason analytically.*

**Sherlock Holmes in *A Study in Scarlet* (1887)**

Criminal or offender profiling as it is now often called, is not a new concept in the fight against crime. Profiling has been around from the Middle Ages with the publication of the book *Malleus Maleficarum* in 1486, a diatribe, supposedly approved by the Roman Catholic Church, which set out methods to identify and eradicate witches. But the concept is constantly evolving and moving in different directions and adopting separate approaches.

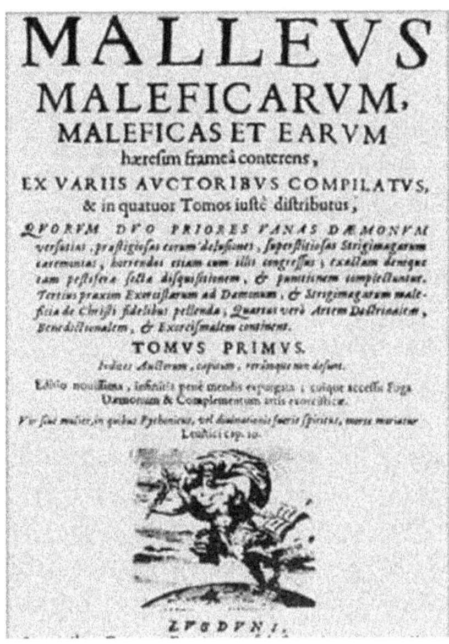
MALLEVS
MALEFICARVM,
MALEFICAS ET EARVM
hæresim frameâ conterens,
EX VARIIS AVCTORIBVS COMPILATVS,
& in quatuor Tomos iustè distributus,
QVORVM DVO PRIORES VANAS DÆMONVM versutias, præstigiosas eorum delusiones, superstitiosas Strigimagarum cæremonias, horrendos etiam cum illis congressus; exactam denique tam pestiferæ sectæ disquisitionem, & punitionem complectuntur. Tertius praxim Exorcistarum ad Dæmonum, & Strigimagarum maleficia de Christi fidelibus pellenda; Quartus verò Artem Doctrinalem, Benedictionalem, & Exorcismalem continent.
TOMVS PRIMVS.
ZVGDVNI.

So, what exactly is criminal profiling? Simply speaking, profiling can be described as the identification of specific attributes of an offender committing a particular crime by a thorough and systematic observational process assisted by an analysis of the crime scene, the victim, the forensic evidence, and the known facts of the crime.

In the area of science three types of professionals can be engaged in the investigation of criminal behavior; behavioral scientists, social scientists, and forensic scientists. But profiling is not exclusively a science; nor is it an art. Hence the dilemma.

In fact, there is still confusion as to the meaning and use of the term "profile". Various agencies use the term to describe different activities. Furthermore, the image of the profiler, as created by popular media such as the motion picture *Hannibal* and television series *Criminal Minds* has so compounded the problem, that this media image has begun to influence some academics about what profiling actually consists of.

To add to this confusion there are even different types of profiling and different approaches to profiling. This book will endeavor to demystify the various terms for you.

Criminal profiling has been referred to, among other less common terms, as behavioral profiling, crimes scene profiling, offender profiling, psychological profiling and criminal investigative analysis (Palermo and Kocsis, 2005).

Some of these terms are interchangeable and some are not. For example, Kocsis, Cooksey, and Irwin (2004), provide their interpretation of criminal psychological profiling. They describe it as a technique used during an investigation whereby crime behaviors are analyzed for identifying possible distinct offender characteristics.

Furthermore there are other types of profiling which are not akin to offender profiling or psychological profiling such as geographical profiling. In the coming chapters we will define the subtle differences in each term with a view to providing the reader with a good overall understanding of the terms involved.

From the early 1950s profiling was predominantly carried out by psychiatrists, psychologists and other mental health professionals. The approach they adopted is called diagnostic evaluation or sometimes the clinical approach.

# 2 DIAGNOSTIC EVALUATION

*How often have I said to you that when you have eliminated the impossible, whatever remains, however improbable, must be the truth?*

**Sherlock Holmes, *The Sign of Four* (1923)**

Diagnostic evaluation is one of the four different approaches to profiling, the other three being Crime Scene Analysis, Investigative Psychology and Geographical Profiling. The chief proponents of diagnostic evaluations would include Dr. James Brussel who was involved in the *Mad Bomber of New York* and the *Boston Strangler* cases.

During the 1950s Freudian psychiatrist Dr. James Brussel provided the NYPD with a criminal profile the fame of which has ensured it will always remain part of offender profiling folklore, partly because of its uncanny accuracy and partly because the case effected an historic turning point for the FBI's future program in profiling.

George P. Metesky (pictured below), better known as the *Mad Bomber*, terrorized New York City for sixteen years in the 1940s and 1950s with explosives and bombs. He planted bombs in terminals, libraries, offices, phone booths, storage lockers, and restrooms in public buildings, including Grand Central Terminal, Pennsylvania Station, Radio City Music Hall, the New York Public Library, the Port Authority Bus Terminal and the RCA Building, as well as in the New York City Subway.

He also bombed movie theaters, where he cut into seat upholstery and slipped his explosive devices inside. Metesky planted a total of thirty three bombs, of which twenty two exploded. While no one ever died in the attacks, fifteen people were injured, some seriously. He was eventually apprehended, based on an early use of offender profiling and clues given in letters he had written to a newspaper. He was found legally insane and committed to a state mental hospital. Who was he? Why did he do it? How was he caught?

## THE MAD BOMBER OF NEW YORK

George Metesky was born in 1904 and was one of four children of an immigrant, Catholic Polish family who lived at number 17 Fourth Street in Waterbury, Connecticut. He enjoyed an unspectacular and happy childhood and was loved by his parents and doted on by his half, older sisters Mary and Anna Milausky, who were daughters of his mother by a previous marriage. Moderately religious, George attended Sunday Mass at St. Patrick's Church, a practice he continued into his adult life. His father who was a timber yard night-watchman, died in 1940 when George was thirty five years old.

George began his campaign on the 16 November 1940. That morning he travelled to midtown Manhattan by public transport carrying a small wooden package. He arrived at the Consolidated Edison building on West 64th Street. He placed the wooden toolbox on a windowsill and then escaped out of the building unnoticed. Consolidated Edison or Con Ed as it is known, was and is, the main supplier of energy for the city of New York. The offices were so huge and full of bustle that nobody took any notice of a stranger.

But the bomb was a dud and was never intended to explode. Metesky had written a note with it in large neat block capitals which read:
*Con Edison crooks, this is for you.*

The bomb was discovered by some employees who alerted the bomb squad. The bomb squad officers found no fingerprints on the device nor any other evidence with which to trace the crudely made device. The note inspired some curiosity, principally because it would have been destroyed if the device had exploded. This meant that the bomb-maker may never have intended the bomb to go off. At least, not this one.

Con Ed and police investigators checked the records of recently dismissed and disgruntled employees who had a grievance against the company. When no suspects surfaced the matter was forgotten about. The incident didn't even make the newspapers. The bomber was offended by this apparent lack of respect but he chose not to react. At least, not right away.

Then, almost a year later, another device was discovered lying on 19th Street. This was a few blocks from Con Edison's Irving Place offices. The device did not go off. Its simple alarm-clock detonator had not been wound. The bomber had wrapped his handiwork in an old woolen sock. This time there was no note.

Even if it was another dud, from another crank, it had to be checked out. The bomb squad investigators recognized the construction as similar to the previous device. They assumed the bomber had been on his way to the Con Edison offices nearby and for some reason had been forced to abort his attempt to plant the bomb. He had simply discarded the device onto the street. Once again the incident didn't make the papers. The papers covered other more important stories like the war in Europe and America's inevitable involvement in the conflict. The war occupied nearly every page, every day.

Three months later, as America entered the war, the bomber sent a letter to Manhattan Police headquarters. Written in neat block letters it read:

> **I will make no more bomb units for the duration of the War. My patriotic feelings have made me decide this. Later I will bring the Con Edison to justice. They must pay for their dastardly deeds.**

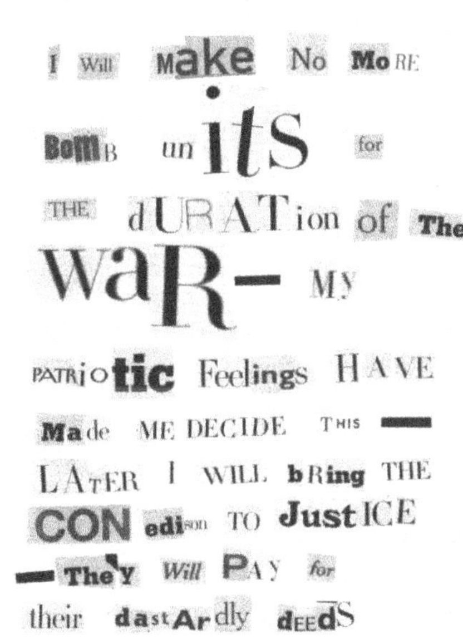

I Will make No MoRE
BomB units for
THE dURATion of The
waR– MY
PATRiotic Feelings HAVE
Made ME DECIDE THIS –
LATER I WILL bRing THE
CON edison TO JustICE
– TheY Will PAY for
their dastArdly dEEdS

The *Mad Bomber* sent other letters over the next nine years signed "F.P." to private citizens, the media, cinemas, Con Edison and the NYPD. The initials "F.P." stood for "Fair Play." True to his word the *Mad Bomber* didn't plant any devices during the war or in the period of truce. But then the terror started in earnest.

On the 29 March, 1951 the new wave of bombing began when a small device exploded in Grand Central Station. It had been dropped into a sand urn near the *Oyster Bar* on the Terminal's lower level. The bomb exploded but no one was injured.

The following month a second bomb exploded without injury in a telephone booth in the New York Public Library. Then in August a phone-booth bomb exploded without injury at Grand Central. He also targeted Con Ed, placing one bomb in a phone booth at their headquarters building at 4 Irving Place and mailing another one to them from White Plains, New York.

Increasingly desperate to receive attention he sent a letter to the New York *Herald Tribune* on the 22 October which read:

> **Bombs will continue until Consolidated Edison Company is brought to justice for their dastardly acts against me. I have exhausted all other means. I intend with bombs to cause others to cry out for justice for me.**

The letter was written in penciled block letters and directed police to the Paramount Theater in Times Square, where a bomb was discovered and disabled, and to a hoax call at a telephone booth at Pennsylvania Station where nothing was found.

In December 1951 the *Herald Tribune* received another warning letter:

> **Have you noticed the bombs in your city – if you are worried, I am sorry – and also if anyone is injured. But it cannot be helped – for justice will be served. I am not well, and for this I will make the Con Edison sorry – yes, they will regret their dastardly deeds – I will bring them before the bar of justice – public opinion will condemn them – for beware, I will place more units under theater seats in the near future. FP.**

Nothing happened for three months and then on the 19 March a device exploded in a phone booth at the Port Authority Bus Terminal without causing injury. In June and again in December bombs exploded in seats at the Lexington Avenue Loew's Theater.

The December bombing injured one person, and was the first Metesky bomb to cause injury. The NYPD had requested an embargo from the media not to publish any of the bomber's letters and to play down the earlier bombings. Even so, the general public were aware that a mad bomber was on the loose.

The campaign continued in 1953 when bombs exploded in seats at Radio City Music Hall and at the Capitol Theater, with no injuries. Another bomb exploded near the *Oyster Bar* in Grand Central Terminal, this time in a coin-operated rental locker but police were beginning to think some of these bombs were copycat devices.

In March 1954, a device edged behind a sink in a Grand Central Terminal men's room exploded injuring three men. Other bombs were reportedly found at the Port Authority and Penn Station and then on the 7 November as a capacity crowd of over 6,000 watched Bing Crosby in *White Christmas*, a bomb which was stuffed into the bottom cushion of a seat, exploded injuring four people and causing mayhem.

The proliferation of bombs continued in 1955 with devices placed on a platform at the IRT Sutter Avenue subway station in Brooklyn, another in *Macy's* department store, two at Penn Station and one at Radio City Music Hall after a warning phone call and at several other locations. None resulted in any serious injuries.

In December 1956 an incident occurred which finally galvanized the NYPD into effective action. New Yorkers seeking to forget their pre-holiday worries filed into the Paramount Movie Theater in Brooklyn.

Some movie-goers were weighed down with Christmas packages obtained in afternoon shopping excursions. Others carried briefcases, the contents of which they hoped to escape for a couple of hours. At 7:55 p.m., a bomb ripped the theater apart.

When the smoke and panic cleared, six people were injured, three of them seriously, one so badly that surgeons spent the night trying to save his life. As the bomber himself would soon write, it was "by the hand of God" that nobody had been killed.

It seemed only a matter of time before somebody would be killed. Meanwhile, the devices were becoming more powerful and sophisticated.

The *Mad Bomber* had now been planting bombs in New York City for sixteen years and the NYPD had no idea who he was. The media began to turn the screw on the police department and demanded action. The public demanded results.

Still the NYPD could not trace the bomber. He never left a trace of evidence on any of his devices; no one had ever seen him; in fact, they didn't even have any suspects. The criticism being levied on the NYPD and the Mayor intensified. Something drastic had to be done; and it had to be immediate.

Since traditional means hadn't worked, Inspector Howard Finney of the New York City crime laboratory decided it was time to try something new. He asked a colleague, Captain Cronin, at the Missing Person's Bureau to assist him with any ideas he might have.

Cronin suggested that perhaps a psychiatrist could build up a profile of the bomber and that the profile might be useful in catching him. After all, Charles Langer had created a profile of Hitler and tried to make predictions about how Hitler would react to defeat.

The problem was that criminal profiling was a nearly new concept and had never been used effectively to solve a major crime case. Cronin recommended Finney talk to a friend of his who had had some minor success in psychiatric detecting. Finney was prepared to go out on a limb. He understood it was a risk but he was determined to try. Finney accompanied by two detectives paid a visit to Cronin's friend a criminal psychiatrist in Manhattan called James Brussel.

## DR. JAMES BRUSSEL

James Brussel, like every other New Yorker, was aware of the case. He had read about it in the newspapers and had himself often wondered what type of person could be responsible for these acts. Primarily in private practice, Dr. Brussel also served as the Assistant Commissioner of Mental Hygiene for the State of New York, a position that led to numerous consultations with police forces and appearances at police conferences. At those conferences, he had both impressed and befriended Captain Cronin. He agreed to help.

Later, in his memoir, *The Casebook of a Criminal Psychiatrist,* Dr. Brussel admits he doubted he could be useful to Finney's case. Despite being confident of his profession and his own abilities, he didn't really think that he could add anything that professional detectives had already discovered.

But his self-doubts were somewhat misplaced. If anyone could effectively profile a criminal, he could. Prior to his private practice, Dr. Brussel had served in the military as chief of Neuropsychiatry at Fort Dix during World War II. He then served as the head of army Neuropsychiatry for the entire army during the Korean War. During that time, he had carried out counterintelligence profiling work for the FBI and the CID.

Brussel also admits that he felt somewhat intimidated by Finney. He felt Finney wouldn't settle for anything but solid conclusions and would dismiss the psychiatric profession entirely if he proved to be wrong. Brussel read the file and came up with a profile. The main conclusion which the detectives had already reached was that the bomber was most certainly mad. But what the police had considered as scant-evidence was a wellspring for Dr. Brussel. After pouring through the case file, he came up with the following conclusions and his reasons for them:

The bomber was male. With a few exceptions, historically bombers have always been male. The bomber had a grudge against Con Edison and was likely a former employee. The widely publicized stories in the press antagonized the bomber.

The bomber was a textbook paranoid. The bomber believed that Con Edison and the public at large conspired against him.

The bomber was middle-aged, probably around 50. Paranoia generally peaks around age 35 and the bomber had been active for 16 years.

The bomber was neat, meticulous and skilled at his work. Everything from the carefully constructed bombs, to the neat lettering, to the careful planning of the bombs indicated his neatness. Also, paranoids tend to set high standards for themselves so as not to open themselves to unwanted criticism.

The bomber was overly sensitive to criticism. This is a classic symptom of paranoia. The bomber was foreign or spent the majority of his time with foreign people. The bomber wrote in stilted, formal language bereft of any contemporary slang. He utilised phrases like "dastardly deeds" that sounded as if they were out of Victorian fiction. He referred to Con Edison as "the Con Edison" when New Yorkers had referred to the utility giant without the article "the" for years.

The bomber had at least a high school education but probably no college. The stilted language of the letters and skilled construction of the bombs spoke of self-education. The excellent handwriting indicated at least some formal schooling.

The bomber was a Slav and probably Roman Catholic. Culturally speaking, Eastern and Central Europeans most often employ bombs as weapons. Most Slavs are Catholic; the bomber lived in Connecticut, not New York. Some of the letters had been mailed from Westchester Country (a location in between Connecticut and New York) and Connecticut was home to large communities of Eastern and Central Europeans.

The bomber suffered from an Oedipal Complex. Like most Oedipal sufferers he was most likely to be unmarried and living with a single female relative or relatives who were not his mother. He probably lost his mother when he was young. Dr. Brussel made these conclusions based on the phallic construction of the bombs; the strange (and breast-like) Ws in the bombers otherwise perfect handwriting and the strange slashing and penetration of the movie theatres seats.

As Finney and his men were leaving, Dr. Brussel stopped them to add one final idiosyncrasy:

> **One more thing, when you catch him, and I have no doubt you will, he'll be wearing a double-breasted suit. And it will be buttoned.**

Although the police policy had been to keep the bomber investigation low-key, Brussel convinced them to heavily publicize the profile. He strongly believed that any wrong assumption made in it would prod the bomber to respond.

Under the headline "Sixteen Year Search for a Madman," the *New York Times* version of the profile summarized the major predictions:

Single man, between 40 and 50 years old, introvert. Unsocial but not anti-social. Skilled mechanic. Cunning. Neat with tools. Egotistical of mechanical skill. Contemptuous of other people.

Resentful of criticism of his work but probably conceals resentment. Moral. Honest. Not interested in women. High school graduate. Expert in civil or military ordnance. Religious. Might flare up violently at work when criticized. Possible motive: discharge or reprimand.

Feels superior to critics. Resentment keeps growing. Present or former Consolidated Edison worker. Probably case of progressive paranoia.

Newspapers published the profile and by the end of the month, bomb hoaxes and false confessions had risen to epidemic proportions.

On the 26 December 1956 the editor of the *American Journal* wrote an open letter to the bomber begging him to give himself up. In return the paper offered to give a full airing to his grievances. The response came two days later. A bomb was placed in a slashed seat in the Paramount Theatre but was made safe by a police bomb disposal team. Like the previous bombs it was an improvised device consisting of a piece of metal piping with nuts at both ends. On that same Friday afternoon the *Journal American* received a reply from the bomber. It read:

> **I read your paper of December 26 - Placing myself in custody would be stupid – do not insult my intelligence – bring the Con Edison to justice – start working on Lehmann – Poletti – Andrews.**

The letter was signed "F.P." The persons named in the reply were the former Governor of New York state, a former lieutenant governor and a former industrial commissioner. The bomber went on to promise a truce until mid-January and he listed the sites of fourteen bombs he had planted in 1956, many of which had still not been discovered. The police found eight bombs, five dummies and three live devices.

Not wanting to stir up public panic the Police Commissioner Stephen P. Kennedy asked the editor of the *American Journal* not to print the letter. Instead the editor placed an advertisement in the personal column of the paper which read:

> **We received your letter. We appreciate the truce. What were you deprived of? We want to hear your views and help you. We will keep our word. Contact us the same way as previously.**

But reporters from other newspapers spotted the item and the secret became public knowledge. The *American Journal* not wishing to be out-scooped on their own story printed the bomber's letter together with another appeal. This resulted in a further communication from the bomber, promising a truce until the 1 March and the offer of an important piece of information.

The information he offered was that he had been injured on a job at the Consolidated Edison plant and although totally and permanently disabled he had not received any kind of assistance from the company.

Metesky's second letter provided some details about the materials used in the bombs (he favored pistol powder, as "shotgun powder has very little power"), and promised a bombing "truce" until at least the 1 March.

He told them he was injured on a job at Consolidated Edison plant as a result of which he was totally and permanently disabled, going on to say that he had had to pay his own medical bills and that Consolidated Edison had blocked his workers' compensation case. He also said:

> **When a motorist injures a dog he must report it, not so with an injured workman. He rates less than a dog. I tried to get my story to the press. I tried hundreds of others. I typed tens of thousands of words (about 800,000). Nobody cared...I determined to make these dastardly acts known. I have had plenty of time to think. I decided on bombs.**

After police editing, the newspaper published his letter on the 15 January and asked the bomber for further details and dates about his compensation case so that a new and fair hearing could be held. On the 19 January the *American Journal* received Metesky's third letter. In it he complained of lying unnoticed for hours on cold concrete after his injury without any first aid being rendered, as a result of which he developed pneumonia and later tuberculosis. The letter included more details about his lost compensation case and claimed that his co-workers had perjured themselves. The accident happened on the 5 September, 1931. He thanked the newspaper for publicizing his case and promised to discontinue the bombings. The letter was published the day after his arrest.

When detectives called to his home at 17 Fourth Street in Waterbury which he shared with his two unmarried sisters they discovered that while he didn't work he drove an expensive, British built Daimler, bought for him by his sisters. Dressed in his bathrobe, he pleasantly and politely confessed to being the bomber. He revealed that F.P. stood for "Fair Play." Detectives searched his house and found a typewriter in one of the bedrooms that forensic examination would later identify as the one that had written the letters. In the garage police found a workshop with a lathe, and a length of pipe used in the bombs.

The police requested that Metesky change clothes before they arrested him. He obliged, and when they took him away he was wearing a double-breasted suit, buttoned. Metesky was examined at Belle Vue mental hospital and considered to be acutely paranoid and incapable of standing trial.

He was committed to Matteawan State Hospital where Dr. Brussel visited him occasionally until his release in 1974. Metesky returned to his home in Waterbury, Connecticut and lived to the ripe old age of 90.

The pursuit of the *Boston Strangler* was equally difficult and brought about a serious division of mental health opinions highlighting, not for the first time, the fallibility and unscientific nature of criminal profiling. A team of experts failed to agree on a likely suspect, often changed their minds on a profile, and couldn't agree if there was one or more suspects involved. The entire episode proved to be a major set back for criminal profiling.

## THE BOSTON STRANGLER CASE

Albert De Salvo was in custody awaiting trial on a series of sexual assaults when he allegedly confided to another inmate that he had killed thirteen women in the Boston area. He then made a detailed confession to the police. Although he was able to give some details of the killings he was not positively identified by a single surviving victim or by any eye witnesses.

Speculation existed then and continued to grow that the killings were the work of more than one man. This is primarily based on the differences in the *modi operandi* of the killings. De Salvo was sentenced to life in prison for his previous crimes. He never actually stood trial for any of the *Boston Strangler killings*. Some experts believe that the man he allegedly confided in, George Nassar, (pictured above) was himself the *Boston Strangler*. But Nassar is not the only suspect. Very recently it has been definitely proved that Albert De Salvo (pictured below) did not murder one of the victims he said he did. Did he lie about the others?

The *Boston Strangler* was the name given to the person or persons who between the 14 June, 1962 and the 4 January, 1964, sexually assaulted and strangled thirteen single women between the ages of 19 and 85 in and around Boston, Massachusetts.

They were assaulted and strangled in their apartments and because there was never any sign of forced entry it was assumed that the victims either knew their assailants or had voluntarily allowed them into their homes. Either that or the killer represented himself as some type of maintenance, delivery or some other service man or maybe even a law enforcement official. The attacks occurred in various suburbs and towns around Boston making overall jurisdiction over the crimes unclear.

After the murder of five women, Anna Slesers, Nina Nichols, Helen Blake, Ida Irga and Jane Sullivan the police noticed a number of startling common denominators:

- All were murdered in the Boston area
- The women were older women between the ages of 55 and 75
- They were white Caucasian
- They all lived alone
- Their apartments were ransacked
- They allowed their intruder in
- The motive was not robbery
- They were all sexually assaulted
- They were all strangled
- The killer's signature was a bow he made with their own clothing
- All bodies were carefully positioned to cause maximum exposure of their sexual organs

No further attacks happened for three months. But people, especially women, spoke of nothing else in the Boston area. What kind of psycho could do such vile disgusting things to these old women? At least younger women were safe from the *Boston Strangler*, weren't they?

Sophie Clarke probably thought so. She lived in Boston. In fact, her apartment was at 315 Huntington Avenue in the Back Bay area which was just a couple of blocks away from Anna Slesers' apartment, the *Boston Strangler's* first victim. But Sophie didn't live alone. She was a student at the Carnegie Institute of Medical Technology and shared her apartment with two roommates. And, she wasn't middle aged like the victims of the *Boston Strangler*.

She was an attractive and popular twenty one year old African American. So, she wasn't his type. She was a student and everyone knows students are broke so there wouldn't be much point in breaking into her apartment to steal anything. It was her roommates who found her.

Sophie's nude body lay with her legs spread wide apart in the living room strangled by three of her own nylon stockings which had been knotted and tied very tightly around her neck. Her half-slip had also been tied around her neck. There was evidence of sexual assault and semen was found on the rug near her body. There was no sign of forced entry. As Sophie was very security conscious she had insisted on having a second lock on the apartment door.

She was so cautious that she even questioned friends that came to the door before she let them in. But she let her killer in. Why? There was evidence of a struggle. The intruder had rummaged through the drawers in the apartment. He then examined her collection of classical records. She had been in the process of writing a letter to her boyfriend when the knock came on the door. She had not dated anyone in the Boston area. In fact, she was quite reserved with the opposite sex.

The police carried out a house to house check questioning all immediate neighbors. Mrs. Marcella Lulka lived in the same apartment building as Sophie. She had an interesting story to tell the police.

At about 2:20 p.m. that afternoon a man calling himself "Mr. Thompson" knocked on her front door. He said the building superintendent had sent him up to see her about painting her apartment. He told her that he would have to repair her bathroom ceiling. He then complimented her on her figure, adding "Have you ever thought of modelling?"

It was a question many women before and after had been asked in the Boston area and they had their own story to tell, but not just yet. She wasn't too impressed. She put her finger to her lips and got rid of him by saying, "My husband is sleeping in the next room." Thompson then said he had the wrong apartment and left, angry, and in a hurry.

When asked to describe Mr. Thompson she said he was between twenty five and thirty years old, of average height and with honey-colored hair. As regards his clothes, he was wearing a dark jacket and dark green trousers. When questioned, the building superintendent said he never sent anyone to check on his tenants.

Sophie Clark had been murdered at or around 2:30 p.m. The police couldn't locate Mr. Thompson but he would soon become a major player in this story.

Patricia Bissette was a twenty three year old secretary for a Boston engineering firm. Her boss called for her early on the morning of the 31 December 1962 but she wasn't at home, so he left. When she didn't turn up for work or call in sick he decided to re-visit her apartment that evening to check on her. Her apartment building was at 515 Park Drive in the Back Bay area. That was the same area in which Anna Slesers and Sophie Clark lived. Patricia's apartment was locked, so her boss, with the help of the superintendent, climbed through a window into the apartment.

They found her body face up in bed with the covers drawn up to her chin, looking like she was taking a nap. However, underneath the covers, she lay there with several stockings knotted and interwoven with a blouse tied tightly around her neck. There was evidence of rape. Patricia was in an early stage of pregnancy.

An examination showed damage to her rectum. The killer had searched her apartment. Nothing happened for a couple of months. During this time the police re-examined the few clues they had desperately trying to find some connection, any connection between the killings. They couldn't find anything.

Lawrence is not a suburb of Boston. It is a city which lies thirty miles north north-west of Boston in Essex County. The composer Leonard Bernstein was born here in August 1918. *Boston Strangler* victim Mary Brown died here in March 1965. Mary Brown was sixty eight years old. She was found beaten to death in her apartment. She had been manually strangled and a fork had been stuck into one of her bared breasts.

There was no evidence of the now famous "Strangler's knot." Because her skull had been beaten to a pulp with a piece of metal piping it was assumed that she had disturbed a burglar and this death was not immediately connected with the Strangler. But was the assumption correct?

The murder scene moved back to Boston two months later. On Wednesday, the 8 May 1963, Beverly Samans, a pretty twenty three year old graduate student, missed choir practice at the Second Unitarian Church in Back Bay. Her friend went to her apartment and opened it with the key she had given to him. The moment he opened the door he put his hand to his face in horror as he saw her body.

She was lying directly in front of him on a sofa bed, her legs spread apart. Her hands had been tied behind her with one of her scarves. A nylon stocking and two handkerchiefs were tied and knotted around her neck. A cloth had been stuffed into her mouth. Although it looked as if she had been strangled.

Beverly had, in fact, died as a result of four stab wounds to her throat. All in all, she had been stabbed a total of twenty two times. Eighteen stabs were in a bull's eye design on her left breast. The ligature around her neck was purely "decorative" or symbolic. It had not been tied tightly enough to strangle her. That was not the killer's intention. The blood stained knife was found in her kitchen sink.

Beverly had been viciously raped. It was estimated that she had been dead approximately forty eight to seventy two hours and had probably been killed between late Sunday evening or Monday morning. She was studying to be an opera singer and had planned to try out for the Met in New York that year.

Police speculated that because of her singing she had developed very strong throat muscles that may have made strangulation more difficult and resulted in her stabbing. But it was just speculation. In fact, it was beginning to appear that that was all the Boston police had in these murders, nothing but speculation.

The police were getting desperate or maybe the police were just desperate. At the time Boston police were best known for one thing, Corruption, with a capital C. Now, they were making a name for themselves as Incompetent, with a capital I. Someone had put the Boston Police Department in touch with an ad copywriter named Paul Gordon. Gordon was supposed to have special ESP qualities. He claimed he knew who the Strangler was and could describe what he looked like. The Boston Police unable to come up with a single lead were more than normally receptive to this untraditional approach.

Gordon was so good he claimed he could even give them an actual profile of the *Boston Strangler*. This was Gordon's profile of Anna Sleser's killer:

> **I picture him as fairly tall, bony hands, pale white skin, red, bony knuckles, his eyes hollow-set. I was particularly struck by his eyes. His hair disturbed me a little because he has a habit of pushing back a little curl of hair that falls on his forehead. He's got a tooth missing in the upper right front of his mouth. He's in a hospital... or some kind of home.**
>
> **He's not confined, I know that, because I see him walking across a wide expanse of lawn. He can walk about, and he does a lot of sitting on a bench on the grounds. He has many problems. He used to beat up his mother cruelly, she was an idiotic, domineering woman, and his two sisters live unhappy lives.**
>
> **The family comes from Maine or Vermont. He's terribly lonely, when he's in the city. I see him sleeping in cellars, but he likes to wander about the street watching women, wanting to get as close as possible to them. You see, the poor fellow is in a continual search for his mother, but he can't find her because she's dead.**

It was not a poor attempt at a criminal profile of the person they might be looking for. One of the detectives brought out a number of photos of men who had been caught mugging or breaking and entering into buildings in the Back Bay area. Sure enough, Gordon identified one of them. His name was Arnold Wallace. He also matched the description that Gordon had given earlier. So, who was this man called Wallace?

Wallace was a twenty six year old mental patient at Boston State Hospital who enjoyed "ground privileges." A few days earlier he had wandered away and was found sleeping in the basement of various apartment houses. He was known to be violent. He had also a history of assaults on his mother. Then the police asked Gordon about the murder of Sophie Clark.

Gordon was able to correctly describe her home in such detail that one would have thought he had been there. He could also describe her killer. He was a large, husky black man who Sophie knew.

The detectives were astounded by the detail in which Gordon described the apartment. Not only that, but the police had a suspect in mind. His name was Lewis Barnett and he fitted Gordon's description to a tee. Barnett and Clark had dated once so it was possible she would have let him into her apartment. Gordon went on to say that the *Boston Strangler* would identify himself soon and confess, adding:

> **And when this fellow confesses, it's going to be like a big carpet rolled out in front of you and all the answers will be so simple you'll kick yourself for months at a time that you couldn't see it.**

It was all so accurate you couldn't make it up. Or could you? When the police went to question Arnold Wallace they were advised that he had escaped from the hospital five or six times. When I say escaped, it was not something like the Escape from Alcatraz. He merely wandered out the gate and didn't turn up for tea. But what was interesting was that his wanderings happened to coincide with the dates on which the *Boston Strangler* had struck. The police brought Gordon to the hospital so that he could see Arnold Wallace in the flesh. "He's the man," declared Gordon. Case solved, time for a coffee and doughnuts? Not exactly.

Detectives decided to look into Gordon's activities before they proceeded any further with Arnold Wallace. They discovered that Gordon had been to the hospital before he had talked to the police. Therefore, it was possible he could have seen Arnold on the grounds.

Maybe the whole thing was a hoax. Or, maybe Wallace was the Strangler. Maybe even Gordon was the Strangler.

Arnold had an IQ between 60-70. So, he was no Nobel Prize contender. He was given a lie detector test. However, his inability to distinguish between fantasy and reality made the tests difficult and inconclusive. He was returned to the hospital, while police tried to check out all of the circumstantial evidence. Even serial killers need a vacation and between May and September 1963 there was a lull in proceedings. That all changed shortly after holiday makers made their way back from Cape Cod.

Evelyn Corbin was a pretty fifty eight year old divorcee who could easily pass for early forties. She lived in Salem, at least she did until the 8 September 1963.

She was found murdered, strangled with two of her nylon stockings. She lay across the bed face up and nude. Her knickers had been stuffed into her mouth to gag her. Lipstick-marked tissues were thrown around the bed. The tissues also contained traces of semen. Forensics found semen in her mouth, and in her vagina.

It appeared obvious that she had been forced to perform oral sex on her attacker. Her locked apartment had been searched, but apparently nothing was stolen. A tray of jewelry had been placed on the floor. The contents of her purse had been emptied onto the sofa. And then there was something surreal. Outside her window on the fire escape, a fresh doughnut, lay there alone waiting to be eaten.

President John Fitzgerald Kennedy was assassinated on the 22 November 1963. While most Americans were glued to their TV sets watching their beloved President and First Lady's arrival in Dallas, Joann Graff was being viciously raped and murdered in her ransacked apartment in Lawrence. Joann was a very conservative and religious twenty three year old industrial designer. The crime scene was something of a familiarity. Two nylon stockings had been tied in an elaborate bow around her neck. Her attacker had bitten into her breast. The outside of her vagina was lacerated and covered with blood.

At approximately 3:25 p.m. on the day of the murder a student who lived upstairs heard footsteps in the hall. His wife had been concerned that someone had been sneaking around in the hallways. She made him go and check. Just then he heard a knock on the door of the apartment opposite his. He opened his door to see a man. He described that man as about twenty seven, with greased hair, dressed in dark green slacks and a dark shirt and jacket.

He asked him a question: "Does Joan Graff live here?" He noticed that he mispronounced Joann's name. The student told him that Joann lived on the floor directly below. The man left. The student, curious, waited. Moments later, he heard the door open and shut on the floor beneath him and assumed that she had let the man into her apartment.

Just ten minutes later a friend telephoned Joann. The phone rang out. The morning before Joann's death, a woman, who lived down the hallway, said she heard someone outside her door. Then she saw a piece of paper being slipped under her door. She watched, mesmerized, as it was being moved from side to side, soundlessly. Then, suddenly, the paper vanished and she heard footsteps. What was the significance of this action?

A month later two young women returned home to their apartment at 44A Charles Street to be met by a horrific vista. They found that their nineteen year old room-mate, Mary Sullivan, had been savagely and grotesquely murdered. Like the other victims Mary had been strangled: first with a dark stocking; over the stocking a pink silk scarf tied with a huge bow under her chin; and over that, another pink and white flowered scarf.

A bright "Happy New Year's" card had been placed against her feet. It got worse: she was in a sitting position on the bed, with her back against the headboard. Thick liquid that looked like semen was dripping from her mouth onto her exposed breasts. A broomstick handle had been rammed three and a half inches into her vagina. As suddenly as they had started the murders stopped. But, yet another strange offender was to make his appearance.

Enough was enough. Certainly people faulted the police for many things, but the reality was that serial killers are very difficult to find, especially smart ones that don't leave clues. In spite of the panic that women experienced all over Boston and its suburbs, the fact was that women were continuing to let the killer or killers into their apartments. The police could only guess whether these women admitted him to their homes because they knew him or because he was able to trick them into letting a stranger inside.

A couple of weeks after the murder of Mary Sullivan, Massachusetts Attorney General Edward Brooke took over control of what was commonly known as the *Boston Strangler* case.

Brooke was not your average law enforcement type; nor was he an ordinary politician. He was a handsome, intelligent and polished professional. He was also, at the time, the only African-American Attorney General in the country.

Even more remarkable was the fact that he was a Republican in a solidly Democratic state. He knew he was putting his career on the line.

If he failed to capture the *Boston Strangler* then his career was effectively over. But he had a plan. A practical plan. A plan that made sense. He meant no disrespect for the Boston police, or maybe he did, but this was an unusual case that spanned five police jurisdictions.

He wanted to put together a group that would coordinate the activities of the various police departments. He wanted to assign permanent staff to the Strangler case that would not be pulled off to work on other crimes. He wanted a free flow of information and an end to petty jealousies between police departments. Finally, he wanted to mollify the press. Two lady reporters, Jean Cole and Loretta McLaughlin, for the *Record-American* had made a crusade out of exposing the Boston Police Department's mistakes, charging them with extreme inefficiency. As I said, it was an eminently practical plan.

He needed someone to steer this group, now called the Special Division of Crime Research and Detection, so he chose his close friend, the Assistant Attorney General John S. Bottomly.

It was inevitable that no matter whom he chose he would be criticized. But, Bottomly was always going to be a controversial choice, primarily because of his lack of experience in criminal law. But what he lacked in experience he made up for in honesty and enthusiasm. The idea was that this was a "non-traditional case" and Bottomly was a man of "non-traditional methods."

Edmund McNamara, the Boston Police Commissioner's response was succinct: "Holy Jesus, what a nutcake." Novelist George V. Higgins who worked for Associated Press at that time went further. He said that he "never heard a reference to Bottomly without the word asshole attached as either a suffix or a prefix. I started to think maybe it was part of the guy's name."

Bottomly's top team consisted of Boston Police Department's Detective Phillip DiNatale and Special Officer James Mellon; Metropolitan Police Officer Stephen Delaney; and State Police Detective Lieutenant Andrew Tuney. Dr. Donald Kenefick headed up a medical-psychiatric advisory committee with several well-known experts in forensic medicine. Two months later, Governor Peabody offered a $10,000 reward to any person who furnished information which directly led to the arrest and conviction of the person who had committed the murders of the eleven "official" victims of the Strangler.

The task force became known as The Strangler Bureau. It had a lot of preliminary work to do before it could hit the ground running. To begin with, it collected, collated, organized and assimilated over thirty-seven thousand pages of material from the various police departments that had been involved in the case. The medical team also had their work cut out. They had the task of developing a criminal profile of the kind of person most likely to commit the murders.

The forensic medical experts saw important differences between the murders of the older women and those of the younger women. Because of this, they thought it was unlikely that one person was responsible for all of the killings. In other words, there were copycats. Bottomly turned to Boston's leading psychiatrists for help. Could they draw up a profile of the man they were looking for? Could they re-create the criminal from the crime scenes, victimology and his *modus operandi*?

## THE PROFILING COMMITTEE

Dr. Donald Kenefick headed up the Profiling Committee. The Committee's official membership consisted of Kenefick from the Law Medicine Research Institute of Boston University; Michael A. Luongo, M.D., Medical Examiner of Suffolk County; James. A Brussel, M.D., Assistant Commissioner, of the Department of Mental Health for the State of New York; Arthur J. Mc Bay, Ph.D., of the Massachusetts Department of Mental Health; Leo Alexander, M.D., Max Rinkel, M.D. both of whom were psychiatrists in private practice; and several other physicians among them one whose specialty included anthropology and who, at the time, preferred to remain anonymous.

The Committee had met at intervals throughout the Spring and Summer of 1964 at Boston University's School of Legal Medicine. Some meeting also took place with high ranking police chiefs. But there was disunity of opinion among the ranks of these physicians, psychoanalysts, psychiatrists, anthropologists and psychologists.

One of the major questions they debated was this: Would the Strangler, driven to kill five elderly women because each represented in his madness the mother he hated and or loved, also be driven to kill twenty year old African American Sophie Clark, twenty three year old Patricia Bissette, twenty three year old Beverly Samans, a very younger looking fifty eight year old Evelyn Corbin, twenty three year old Joann Graff and nineteen year old Mary Sullivan? Or were the second set of women, the younger ones, killed by someone else who added scarf-like decorations and elaborate staging to make the killings look as if they were killed by the same person?

In his report Kenefick stated that the majority of the committee agreed that one man probably had killed the first group of older women whom they described as the "Old Women."

He would be "Mr. S. – the Strangler." As to the other group, "the Girls", they probably were not slain by Mr. S. but by one or more men, likely to be found in the circle of the girl's acquaintances, most probably "unstable members of the homosexual community" who had tried to make their acts resemble the stranglings of the Old Women as reported in the newspapers.

The report made sense.

As to the character of the man or men responsible, Kenefick pointed out that he and his colleagues could only hazard a few guesses towards a "common profile." Generally, he explained, the sex murderer contains within himself:

> **an encapsulated core of rage directed at an important figure in his early life, usually a dominant overwhelming female. To cope with his rage, he engages in powerful, sadistic fantasies in which he kills this figure. He differs from other psychotic killers in that he is able to keep his terrible daydreams to himself; exhibiting no odd behavior which would tend to give him away.**

The chances were that he might appear bland, pleasant, gentle, ingratiating, even compassionate. Because of the training given to him by the hated and or loved matriarchal figure he would most likely be neat, punctual, polite, in brief the personality often seen in confidence tricksters, homosexuals and in many normal lower middle class men. No one who knew him would regard him as "crazy."

On the question of what would trigger him to act this way they thought that certain stresses were probably too much for him to cope with.

These might include the death of his mother, or something which caused him to lose self-esteem such as being fired from his job, or anything that made him feel a loss of masculinity.

He was most likely to find himself in a deep depression from which he could only emerge by a sudden, violent explosion of hate involving the murder and destruction of the terrifying female image in a ritualistic killing which would be both sadistic an loving. But because each murder solved nothing for him the murders would continue.

They profiled his likely mother as:

> **a sweet, orderly, neat, compulsive, seductive, punitive, overwhelming woman. She might go about half exposed in their apartment, but punish him severely for any sexual curiosity.**

The chances were that the killer once lived with a woman possessing characteristics similar to those of his victims, and in a similar environment. He was not close to his father who had probably died or deserted the family before his puberty.

In Kenefick's opinion:

> **The boy grew up to feel that women were a fearful mystery. He was inhibited heterosexually but the overwhelming respectability of his background probably kept him from much overt homosexuality.**

Kenefick stated that each time the Strangler killed

> **he was trying to re-establish a seductive scene, to carry out buried incestuous fantasies, and to exorcise certain fears by acting out a fantasy of degrading and controlling an overwhelming and fearsome mother.**

He didn't think that Mr. S was any kind of exceptional man in appearance, not too tall, not too short, not too deformed, or someone would have noticed. He might have conned his way into the apartments or simply slipped the lock. He went on to make the following comments in relation to the manner of killing:

> **It is an easy matter to strangle someone from behind, enough to induce unconsciousness with a forearm grip...he would be at least thirty, perhaps older; strong enough to carry or pull heavy women about the room; neat an orderly; probably single, separated or divorced; a man who knew how to kill efficiently, who was attracted by neat, pleasant old women, with firm complexions and firm flesh...who felt a certain savage titillation in exposing women, who left them with a grotesque imitation of scarves, often elaborately tied around the necks; who contemptuously injure their sexual parts with a fantasy phallus or glass or wood (whose firmness and bigness revealed his wishes and fears)**

> **who looked for some small object; money? photographs? in desks, closets an bureau drawers.**

Kenefick thought the police should concentrate on men whose work was slack in the Summer, Christmas and holiday seasons since most of the attacks occurred around that time.

One interesting observation he made was that the murders took place in what he called "mixed lace curtain Irish, lower drawer Yankee, student type neighborhoods" but despite the fact that the Italians were one of the biggest ethnic groups in Boston no Italians had been targeted.

Why did the murders stop after Mary Sullivan on the 4 January 1964? Was he arrested on another charge? Did he commit suicide? Was he sent to a mental institution? Was he now frightened about being caught? The famed Dr. James Brussel proposed his own theory.

He thought the killer would be in his early thirties or forties, perhaps of Southern European or Spanish stock because garroting was associated with such backgrounds. He believed that:

> **Each killing is a psychotic act committed by a man searching for his potency. As he said, he was an ancient story of the Oedipus complex, a man's unconscious sexual desire for his mother; an impulse he dares not yield to. But each time he approached another women he found he was impotent because his sex drive was fixed upon his mother.**

The killer dealt with this problem in a demented manner because he himself was demented. He needed to destroy his mother's image to free himself from her control and regain his libido.

Brussel believed he stalked and killed Anne Slesers because she resembled his mother.

But after killing her he discovered, much to his surprise, that he was still impotent. He was now enraged. So he assaulted her sexually with an object. He then strangled his second mother image, Helen Blake, who again looked like his mother. But again the killing did not enhance his libido and so it continued.

One of the matters considered by the anthropologist on the committee was that the Old Women resembled each other and if they resembled the killer's mother, then would the killer be found to resemble his victims?

But why then did he suddenly switch from attacking older women to younger attractive women? When he attacked twenty year old Sophie Clark he found for the first time he was now potent. Police found semen there and at the crime scenes of all the younger women. He stopped killing, Brussel suggested because he was "cured." Brussel accepted that he was sticking his neck out with this suggestion and his findings were put into a minority report.

Despite all the work carried out by the Committee it didn't help to catch the killer. It was a blow for the rising star of profiling. They needed something else. Something that would work. It was Bottomly's suggestion and Brooke finally consented to it.

## THE PSYCHIC PETER HURKOS

As the criminal profiling panel couldn't crack the case they decided to involve the well-known Dutch psychic Peter Hurkos (pictured below being interviewed). His official website describes him in the following terms:

> **Peter Hurkos is considered by experts to have been the world's foremost psychic! Born May 21, 1911, in Dordrecht, Holland (died June 1, 1988 in Los Angeles, CA) is celebrating his centennial birthday in 2011, he acquired his psychic gift in 1941 after falling from a ladder and suffering a brain injury... he discovered he had developed an ability to pierce the barriers that separate the past, present and future.**

One cannot but be reminded about what novelist George V. Higgins had said earlier about Bottomly! Two private groups paid for Hurkos' services and expenses. He was a difficult person to work with and ultimately got into difficulty for allegedly impersonating an FBI agent.

To cut a long story short, Hurkos did identify a suspect, one who the Strangler Bureau had already investigated. The suspect was a shoe salesman with a history of mental illness. However, there was no evidence whatsoever to link the shoe salesman with any of the murders. Eventually, the man committed himself to an institution. It would not be unfair to say that the Strangler Bureau's credibility suffered on account of the involvement of Mr. Hurkos.

It was purely by chance that Albert de Salvo was arrested and admitted to being the *Boston Strangler*. Whether or not he was or whether or not he acted alone we don't yet know but we do know that the popularity of profiling as a science had taken a severe hit.

## LIMITATIONS OF DIAGNOSTIC EVALUATIONS

It was inevitable that following the high profile failure in the *Boston Strangler* case that there would be a distancing from psychiatric based profiling and a drift back to solid detective work. But the FBI saw the merits in both and were to play the leading role in the development of modern day criminal profiling.

Profiles described here as "diagnostic evaluations" are the precursors of what today is termed criminal personality profiling. Basically these involve profiles carried out by individual psychiatrists and psychologists as needs arise or as their research interests demand.

The difficulty with diagnostic evaluations is that they do not comprise a unified discipline nor follow any specifically prescribed methodology. Instead, they comprise of a cumulative body of work by individual mental health professionals who are consulted by law enforcement personnel and asked to provide whatever insights they can to seemingly insoluble crimes (Felman 1993). Felman says that:

> **Diagnostic evaluation relies largely on the clinical judgment of a profiler to ascertain the underlying motives behind an offender's action.**

It is from the work of this loose collection of psychiatrists and psychologists that the term 'psychological profiling' was first derived. However, those mental health professionals involved in conducting diagnostic evaluations rarely, if ever, have any extensive experience in law enforcement or related areas. Usually they are solely employed to construct a profile of a likely suspect and accordingly they tend to lack experience (Dietz 1985).

The evaluations are usually based on clinical practice as well as being drawn from knowledge of personality theories and various psychological disorders. Nevertheless, the procedure is quite firmly cemented in the disciplines of psychology or psychiatry. Ressler and Schactman (1992) advise that this esoteric approach is gradually becoming more formalized so as to allow for replication.

The way the system works is that profiles are constructed by diagnosing the probable psychopathology and or personality type of the probable offender. The problem here is that, because of the diverse nature of these profiles and the variability of their accuracy levels, such a diagnosis can vary widely among different practitioners and produce what Goodwin (1978) calls a characterization of criminal personality profiling as "hit and miss" or as Vorpagel (1982) says, it is art not science.

Despite this, some of the most celebrated and accurate profiles have emanated from this approach. So much so that Wilson and Seaman (1992) suggest that their success has yet to be rivalled in detail by practitioners of the other approaches.

However, the fact remains that the majority of profiles produced have been flawed. Examples include Jack the Ripper (Rumbelow 1988), US President Woodrow Wilson (Tuchman 1967), Adolf Hitler (Langer 1972) and the Boston Strangler (Frank 1966). Similar profiles conducted more recently and in Australia include: the Rydlemere Rapist, the Mosman Granny Killer and Mr. Stinky cases (see Simpson & Harvey 1994; Kennedy & Whittaker 1992).

However, it would seem that the type of profiling that we call "diagnostic evaluations" has some measure of success in terms of the profile outcome. As Wilson, Lincoln, and Kocsis (1997) state:

> **While no longer the sole source of offender profiles, diagnostic evaluations by individual psychiatrists, psychologists and criminologists continue to prevail.**

They appear to dominate in most countries in terms of prevalence and they provide the greatest accessibility in terms of the technique involved, one practitioner's knowledge of personality types and information about the crimes provided by police.

However, this individualistic approach also prevents adequate comparative assessments of validity, utility and process, and the category of profiling now in the ascendancy is that of crime scene analysis.

This psychodynamic approach to profiling is based on the clinical experience of the practitioner and is necessary to make accurate predictions (Turco, 1990). Turco produced a four step model based around the notion that all violent behavior was a manifestation of the mother-child struggle, where female victims were representations of all the negative elements of the mother. In the first step, the profiler considers the crime in its entirety, looking for the underlying psychodynamic processes.

In the second step, the profiler assesses the crime scene for any signs of a neurological or brain disorder.

Thirdly, the profiler then analyses the crime scene in terms of the separation-individuation phase of the offender.

Finally, in an effort to construct and compose a profile of unsub, he analyzes the demographic characteristics of the offender and victim.

Copson et al (1997), in an attempt to set out a more systematic approach to profiling compared their individual methodology and produced what they called:

> **A series of steps and sets of features, principles and dangers which...other clinical profilers might care to subscribe to.**

From this, they developed a ten step procedural model with the centerpiece of the model being the inference of motive, which is seen as the key to understanding the offender. They state that the inferred motive:

> **allows the importation of factors from relevant literature as starting points for the development of suggested offender characteristics.**

Copson et al (1997) posit that each piece of advice should be:

Custom Made: The advice should not rely on the recycling of some kind of generic violent anti-social criminal stereotype;

Interactive: At a range of levels of sophistication, depending on the officers' understanding of the psychological concepts at issue; and

Reflexive: The advice should be dynamic, in so far as every element has a knock-on effect on every other element, and evolving, in that new information must lead to reconsideration not only of the elements of advice directly affected but of the construct as a whole.

## THE TEN STEP PROCEDURAL MODEL

Adapted from Copson et al., 1997

1. Receive briefing

2. Request case material depending on the nature of the case

3. Infer reconstruction of events

4. Visit crime scene

    • WHAT (in minute detail)

    • HOW (in minute detail)

    • TO WHOM (in minute detail)

5. Infer motive Allows importation of factors from relevant literature

6. Develop psychological constructs relating back to what/how/to whom

7. Introduce demographic and social factors

8. Generate a range of elements of advice with probability markers as appropriate.

9. Discuss with investigating officer

10. Produce report

## OTHER CRITICISMS

As we know, subsequent dangers remain inherent in the principles and approach of clinical profiling. The wish and indeed need to succeed can result in an undermining of objectivity, while the close interaction between the profiler and law enforcement officers is best avoided in order to avoid any danger that the subsequent profile was developed to fit an already known suspect. As well as this, it is not only desirable but really essential that all data and information be recorded, even though this is an extremely difficult and time-consuming process.

Related to this point, is the failure to produce a summary document of the amassed information, thereby leaving the profile vulnerable to potential misinterpretation (Copson et al., 1997).

While, Copson et al. (1997) lay out a decent model to follow, the problem with it is that it fails to identify a systematic process for the derivation of inferences as this is dependent on the individual clinician. What they actually have produced is a sound set of principles and dangers, which have relevance in providing behavioral investigative advice.

Clarke and Canter (2000) provide a descriptive example of the clinical approach, as applied to sexual murderers. They identified four types of sexual murderers through their work with a sample of UK sexual offenders residing in a specialized treatment center in Brixton Prison in London, UK.

Their profiles for types of sexual murderer were as follows:

1. Sexually motivated murderer, engages in sophisticated and detailed masturbatory fantasies of killing unknown but specifically targeted victims, and who can be clearly seen as the sadistic type with a primary motivation to kill;

2. Sexually triggered murderer, who commits an aggressive, yet controlled murder, which uses killing as a means to keep the victim quiet and to avoid later detection.

3. Grievance motivated murderer, who commits an aggressive and uncontrolled murder but who has no prior intent to kill, yet does so because of something the victim does or says during the assault. Extreme violence and/or humiliation against the victim, usually taking a sexual theme (e.g., mutilation to the genitals), will be evident, suggesting a loss of control.

4. Neuropsychological dysfunction sexual murderer, which was developed around the unclear motivations of one offender who exhibited clear neuropsychological deficits, and does not necessarily depict a group of sexual offenders.

As we can see this clinical approach to profiling is heavily reliant on clinical judgment, training, knowledge, experience, and/or intuition, with the methods used varying according to the individual practitioner (Alison et al., 2010).

The primary focus is on the specific details of each particular case. Profilers of this approach see each case as unique and believe they should be treated as such (Boon, 1997). As a result, this individualistic clinical approach leaves very few models to assess its scientific merit (Muller, 2000) and this is where the main problem lies.

It is primarily based on the individual clinician's experience and knowledge gained through working with individual clients, and the application of this to drawing conclusions or inferences from crime scene information.

And while Copson et al. (1997), and to a lesser extent Turco (1990), provide the building blocks of providing investigative advice, they still fail to explicitly provide guidance on how to specifically construct an actual profile.

As Alison, Goodwill, Almond, van den Heuvel, and Winter (2010) point out the difficulty is:

> **How to judge when and how a clinician's tacit knowledge gets translated into formalized, explicit, and falsifiable knowledge, as well as how this knowledge subsequently leads to the generation of useful offender profiles.**

This is a limitation resulting from the fact that the inferences in this type of clinical approach profiling are made through the knowledge and experiences of the particular clinician (Alison, Goodwill, & Alison, 2005). This not only prejudices the ability to compare this approach with other approaches but also the ability to compare within the clinical approach itself, for example, between cases.

Critics of this approach have also identified another problem relating to what is known as the Barnum or the Forer effect (Forer, 1949). Allow me to explain these terms first.

Snyder, Jae Shenkel, and Lowery (1977) describe the Barum effect as the phenomenon whereby people willingly accept personality interpretations comprised of vague statements with a high base-rate occurrence in the general population.

Snook et al. (2008) describe the Forer effect as the tendency for people to judge general, universally valid statements about personality as specific to themselves.

According to Snook, Cullen, Bennell, Taylor, and Gendreau (2008) people often assume the description provided of the sexual offender is based on a psychological assessment procedure, even if one has not been provided, and are therefore more inclined to accept it.

A large amount of the profiles provided by these approaches are regarded by some as ambiguous and appear to describe any suspect (Alison et al., 2003; Alison, Smith, et al., 2003).

Added to this personal validation effect, is the suggestion that exposure to ambiguous descriptions may increase the faith in psychological assessment methods and the perceptions of the individual clinician's views. This can occur even if the method is not valid or the profiler is not actually skilled (Snook et al., 2008).

Basically, its critics claim the approach is prejudiced by ambiguity and that this ambiguity can also be seen to support a confirmation bias, in which those using the profile may 'notice' or look for information contained within the profile that confirms their preconceptions or hypotheses.

The danger here as pointed out by Snook et al. (2008) is that this has obvious implications if a criminal is then later apprehended, as any ambiguous information contained within the profile, may appear to retrospectively describe them. That has to be our man because he fits the profile instead of that has to be our man because the evidence stacks up against him and he also comes within the profile provided.

# 3 CRIME SCENE ANALYSIS APPROACH

*The problem with putting two and two together is that sometimes you get four, and sometimes you get twenty-two.*

**Dashiell Hammett, *The Thin Man* (1934)**

The 1970s witnessed an increasing prevalence of bizarre and apparently random violent crime. It was the proliferation of this violent crime that prompted the FBI Behavioral Science Unit to commence its own research into offender profiling (Depue 1986; Pinizzotto1984).

But rather than continue with the diagnostic/clinical approach utilized by mental health practitioners, the FBI, being essentially a law enforcement agency, adopted a more utilitarian approach (Ressler, Douglas, Groth and Burgess 1980).

It focused on studying crime scenes and on interviewing violent offenders who were already incarcerated in an attempt to construct typologies for certain offender categories.

From the recognizable patterns in *modi operandi* (Ressler, Burgess & Douglas 1988), together with the baseline data of offender characteristics in conjunction with specific crime scene indicators, the FBI managed to produce reasonably well-defined offender templates.

Before we delve in the academic nuances of this approach let's look at some of the case studies which utilized the crime scene analysis approach. Three particular cases soundly illustrate the use by the FBI of the Crime Scene Analysis approach to profiling; Richard Trenton Chase, Dennis Rader and Gary Ridgway.

## THE RICHARD TRENTON CHASE CASE

*These murders were not ordinary or common. They betrayed a depravity that is so great that the level of reprehensibility manifested is difficult to imagine, almost beyond human conception or imagination.*

**Prosecutor Ronald Tochterman.**

Richard Trenton Chase aka the *Vampire of Sacramento* was an American schizophrenic serial killer and necrophiliac who killed and cannibalized six people between December 1977 and January 1978 in Sacramento,

California and then drank their blood.

Rick was born in Santa Clara County, California on the 23 May 1950 nine months after his parents Richard Sr. and Beatrice married. His father was a computer specialist at McClellan Air Force Base while his mother was a teacher. He was part of the American Baby Boom generation living in the new America, after World War Two, which was filled with hope, opportunity and prosperity.

His sister Pamela was born in 1953 and that year the family moved into their first house in Kings Way, Sacramento. They stayed there until 1961 when due to financial difficulties they were obliged to sell up.

The forced sale of their first family home exacerbated the existing friction which had developed between his parents. They moved into a duplex on Valkyrie Way for two years before buying their second house in Montclaire Street.

While they lived in Montclaire Street, Beatrice believed that her husband was a dope abuser and was unfaithful to her. This led to frequent arguments and it may well be that this adversely affected Rick. By 1963 he was already showing signs of schizophrenia and severe psychosis.

It was also around this time, when he was thirteen, that Rick began to believe he was one of the Younger Brothers. The James-Younger brothers were an infamous gang of outlaws in the Wild West. Rick bought posters of them and wanted to dress like them.

This obsession seemed to have faded after a year when in 1964 he entered Mira Loma High School. Outwardly he appeared normal enough and interacted well with his fellow students, male and female. Teachers remember him as being well-groomed and not unpopular although his grades were poor and continued to get progressively worse. Despite this he managed to graduate in 1968 and his parents bought him a VW Beetle.

In September 1968 Rick enrolled at American River College until the Spring semester of 1971, and then "took a leave of absence." During this time he realized that he was suffering from erectile dysfunction and is known to have seen a psychiatrist in 1969 for help with the problem. Meanwhile he took up a couple of menial jobs but could never keep them for any period of time as he had become addicted to drugs and alcohol.

In 1971 he left home and moved into a house at 3831 Anadale Lane with

Cyd Evans DeMarchi and Rachel Statum. Little did they know what they were letting themselves in for. But they soon found out. Within a matter of days they noticed that Rick was constantly "stoned."

They described him as "uncooperative, inconsiderate, and difficult to be with." He exhibited classic symptoms of paranoia including boarding up the door to his room and knocking a hole in the closet wall to enable him enter and exit his room. Obsessed with "someone trying to sneak up on him" his fellow tenants had enough after they found out he had waved a gun at one of their friends who came to visit them. They asked him to move. He refused so they left only to be replaced by Rachel Statum's brothers and some of their friends all of whom were in a rock band. Rick insisted on joining the band even though he was hopeless.

His behavior at this time became increasingly bizarre and he was accustomed to walking around the apartment butt naked while they were entertaining visitors. Eventually, they threw him out and he moved back with his mother on Montclaire Street. By this time, his parents had separated and divorced.

After a short stint in Los Angeles he returned home to Sacramento. Here he lived with both his mother at Montclaire Street and his father in the duplex on Valkyrie Street. During this period both parents noticed that Rick became obsessed with his state of health. He told his mother, Beatrice, that his head was hurting; his head was changing shape; there was something wrong with his nervous system; that his heart was stopping; that there was something wrong with his blood circulation and that he was afraid he was going to die.

Matters came to a head when on the 1 December 1973 Rick walked into the emergency room at American River Hospital. Here he told them he couldn't breathe; he'd "lost his pulmonary vein;" was suffering from "cardiac arrest;" that "someone had stolen his pulmonary artery and his blood flow had stopped." Dr. Irwin Lyons was assigned to assess him.

He recorded that he was "tense, nervous, and wild-eyed" and was a "filthy, disheveled, deteriorated, and foul-smelling white male." He wasn't sure if Rick was abusing drugs so his diagnosis was "chronic paranoid schizophrenia, acute, though the possibility of a toxic psychosis consequent to ingestion of psychotomimetic drugs cannot be ruled out…"

The doctor also considered Rick's mother to be "highly aggressive, hostile and provocative" quickly adding she was the "so-called schizophrenic mother." On her insistence they let him go. Dr. Lyons' final diagnosis was that Rick was suffering from "chronic paranoid Schizophrenia." He prescribed drugs and for a while they seemed to be working fine.

But by 1976 Beatrice noticed that a sadistic streak had crept into Rick's behavior. He began harming the family's pets. Later he moved into a cottage provided by his father in Cannon Street and for a while kept it clean and in order.

All was well until the 26 April 1976 when Rick was admitted to the Community Hospital in northern Sacramento after he injected himself with rabbit blood. They kept him in for observation. Then on the 28 April they transferred him to American River Hospital, where he remained until the 19 May 1976. He was eventually released on the 29 September 1976. Big mistake number one.

Doctors can't keep patients forever and once they show improvement and their prescribed drugs appear to be working then they actually have a duty to release them. It's a delicate balance between the rights of Society and the rights of the individual. But, no one, could have foreseen the carnage that was about to unfold.

After leaving Beverly Manor his parents were to act as conservators as Rick was not competent to look after himself. The first thing they did was to set him up in apartment. It was number 12 at 2934 Watt Avenue.

Soon Beatrice began to notice that the medication he was taking had the effect of making him into a "Zombie." She didn't consider that this was beneficial for his ongoing development so she took a unilateral decision, without consultation with anyone else, to wean him off his medication. Big mistake number two.

By January 1977 he was living alone; had ceased his medication; and had no follow-up visits with physicians, psychiatrists, psychologists, counsellors or anyone else. He was now left completely to his own devices.

On the 18 December 1977 Rick walked into the Big 5 Sporting Goods shop and collected a Stoeger Arms, Luger-style .22 caliber pistol he had ordered two weeks previously. He also bought a fifty round box of ammunition. The day after Christmas, he purchased an additional box of ammunition. He had gone through the animal stage; he was now ready to kill humans.

He didn't have anyone particular in mind. Anyone would do. At the time,

Bianchi and Buono were two serial killers known as the *Hillside Stranglers* who were operating not far from where he lived. Rick became obsessed with their crimes. We will never know for sure if this was the catalyst that triggered his murder spree.

Rick Chase decided he would drive around his neighborhood and shoot some of his neighbors. His drive by shootings began on the 25 December and continued for over a week. Various people heard the gunshots but no one knew who had fired them.

At 6:30 p.m. on the 27 December a Mrs. Polenske who lived in Lynn Way was busy cleaning her kitchen presses when a single bullet smashed through the window, whizzed through her hair and slammed into the wall.

Two days later on the 29 December, 1977, fifty one year old engineer Ambrose Griffin who was married with two children was helping his wife bring the groceries into their house on Roberston Avenue from their car. Chase drove by and shot him twice, killing him instantly. No one knows why.

On the 7 January 1978 Hugh K. Phares, an instructor at American River College, who lived with his wife, Marguerite, at 3804 Robertson Avenue, reported that someone had fired shots through his window.

Police had no motive for the crimes and the victims were not related or connected. They had no suspects. They had no witnesses. They had no clues. And things were about to get worse, much worse.

God only knows what went through the mind of Richard Trenton Chase when he awoke on Monday the 23 January 1978. A month earlier he had shot dead an innocent man in a drive by shooting. It was almost death by remote control. He sat in his car and pointed the gun. There were phut-phut sounds. Mr. Griffin fell. Chase drove on. He didn't even see a trickle of blood. Today would be different. Today would be personal. Today there would be blood and lots of it.

Twenty two year old Teresa Wallin was an attractive married woman who was three months pregnant. She lived at 2630 Tioga Way with her husband David. As she was putting out the trash that morning she was accosted by Chase who was wielding a .22 caliber pistol. He aimed it at her head. Seeing the weapon she instinctively put her hand up to shield herself. Chase shot her three times.

The first bullet passed through her hand near the wrist and grazed her head. The second entered her cheek and broke her jaw. The final bullet struck her brain and lodged there, rendering her unconscious but still breathing.

As she lay on the living room floor, Chase put on a pair of rubber gloves and dragged her body into a rear bedroom. He shoved her sweater and bra above her breasts and then pulled her pants and panties down to her ankles. He spread her legs to expose her pubic region. He then went to the kitchen to search for a suitable knife. He picked a knife and an empty yoghurt carton.

When he returned he bent over the young mother to be and began to mutilate her. Chase concentrated on specific organs. He cut the pancreas in half; cut the spleen completely out of her body; cut the liver; pulled out the intestines; excised the kidneys and replaced them in different parts of the body; sawed off a portion of the lower left lung; and made several stab wounds to the heart.

While engaged in this work he cupped blood from the body to fill the empty yoghurt cup and then drank from it, several times until the cup was empty. Her warm blood excited him further and he ripped the knife through her left breast "once superficially, once through the nipple and on through to the lung, thrusting the knife three times through the wound."

He stopped for a moment and went to the back yard where he searched for and found some dried dog feces. He brought this back into the house and shoved it into Teresa's mouth. He then retreated to the bathroom to wash his gloves and wipe the knife with a scarf. He placed the knife under some washed dishes.

He left by the back door, went home, turned on the television and looked forward to reading all about it in the *Sacramento Bee* newspaper the following day.

David Wallin never recovered from the sight he witnessed on his return home that night. He rang his father and the police who arrived shortly afterwards. He could never understand why his life changed so dramatically that day. No one could.

It was so brutal that the FBI were called in, and it gave the profilers a chance to show what they were worth. Agents Robert Ressler and Russ Vorpagel developed independent profiles, and both wrote about this case in their respective books.

Ressler (pictured above) says it was the first time he was able to go on-site with a profile, and he was ready. He offers a step-by-step method analysis for how he derived the traits he lists. For example, from a psychiatric study of body type and mental temperament he had read, he decided the offender was scrawny.

Given the disorder at the scene, it was likely that the unsub did not have a career or much education, nothing that required organized thinking and concentration. The profile was all a matter of logic and knowledge about principles of human behavior, which Ressler was able to fully explain to anyone who asked. Vorpagel's profile was similar.

Ressler figured the unsub for a disorganized killer as opposed to an organized one, with clues pointing toward the possibility of paranoid psychosis. He clearly had not planned the crime and did little to hide or destroy evidence. He left footprints and fingerprints, and had probably walked around oblivious to the blood on his clothing. In other words, he gave little thought to the consequences.

His domicile would be as sloppy as the place he had ransacked, and his mental capacity was likely screwed up. That meant he probably did not drive a car, indicating he lived in the vicinity of the crimes. He was white, 25-27, thin, undernourished, lived alone, and probably had evidence that pointed to the crime in his home. He was likely to be unemployed and the recipient of disability money.

All of this was derived from known information that such crimes tended to be intra-racial, specific to a certain age range, and similar to other people with a paranoia-based mental illness. From what Ressler knew, it was also likely that this offender would kill again, and keep on killing until he was caught. They had to work fast.

The Miroth residence at 3207 Merrywood Drive was a modest ranch style house owned by divorced thirty six year old Evelyn Miroth. Evelyn lived there with her two sons, thirteen year old Vernon, and six year old Jason. She didn't work outside of the home but did on occasions babysit her young twenty two month old nephew David Michael Ferreira.

On the morning of the 27 January she was up early and around 7:00 a.m. her sister-in-law Karen dropped David off as she did every Friday morning. She also had a visit from her boyfriend, fifty year old Daniel Meredith.

At approximately 8:30 a.m. a neighbor, Neone Grangaard, who lived across the road called Evelyn to ask her if Jason could join her and her two daughters for a trip to the mountains that day. Then at 9:05 a.m. Evelyn called back asking if they could wait until about 10:00 a.m. to give her time to purchase snow shoes for Jason.

Grangaard said that was fine and at 9:30 a.m. Neone noticed that Karen's boyfriend, Daniel Meredith, had parked his car in Karen's driveway.

Twenty-five minutes later, she watched Dan get back into his car and drive away. By 10:30 a.m. she noticed his car was back, but Dan had already gone back inside the house. Of course, 10:00 a.m. came and went and there was no sign of Jason walking across the street to join the Grangaard family for the outing. Furthermore, by the time Dan had re-entered the house, her phone calls were not being answered.

The whole street was buzzing in general that morning and the Miroth house was buzzing in particular. If Rick Chase had wanted to pick a quiet house he hadn't; in fact, he had chosen one of the most active houses in the neighborhood that particular morning.

Police reports show conflicting times but what we know for certain is that early that morning Chase parked his car at the Country Club Center. He was wearing an orange jacket his father had just bought him and carrying the .22 caliber Luger pistol and a pair of rubber gloves. When he saw only one car at the Miroth residence he entered through an unlocked door, probably through the garage.

He immediately came upon Evelyn Miroth in the hallway and startled her. He shot her in the head. The bullet entered her brain and she fell unconscious and bleeding on the hall carpet. Her son Jason wasn't there. Dan had brought him to the store to buy his snow shoes. But the child David Ferreira was there and was lying asleep in his crib. Chase entered the room and seeing the sleeping child shot him in the head.

He then carried the dead child to the bathroom. He dangled him over the bathtub while he gouged out a section of his brain with a knife and having drained some blood from his head, he drank it. He then mutilated the child's body by stabbing him in the anus.

At some stage, his depravity was interrupted by the arrival of Dan Meredith together with Evelyn's son Jason. As they entered the front room Chase shot Dan in the head. He then shot at Jason. His first shot hit him in the back of the neck and the second in the head. He then shot a second bullet into Dan's head to make sure he was dead.

Believing that he had now murdered everyone who either lived in the house or was calling to it that morning, he then turned his attention to Evelyn. He dragged her from the hallway into the bedroom and striped her naked. He then took most of his own clothes off, picked up the knife and began desecrating her body. He later dragged her to the bathroom pitched her body over the bathtub and sodomized her. He then dragged her back to the bedroom.

The following is a list of some of her injuries. He cut a cross into her abdomen; slashed her liver four times; pulled out some of her stomach; cut into her anus and up into her rectum followed by several stabbings to her uterus. At one stage he thrust the knife back and forth into her rectum. All of these injuries occurred while she was still alive or just dying. Post mortem injuries included eight slashes to the neck after which he gouged out her right eye. Later lab reports confirmed that a significant amount of Chase's sperm was found in Evelyn's rectum.

It was now 11:05 a.m. and neighbor Neone Grangaard was wondering what was going on in the Miroth home that was delaying Jason. Completely unaware of the carnage that was taking place she sent her six-year-old daughter Tracy over to house. Tracy knocked on the door to get in.

Chase, unaware that the person trying to gain entry was just a six year old girl, began to panic. Meanwhile, Tracy walked back to her own house and told her Mum there was no one there.

Ms. Grangaard looked across the road, saw the cars and phoned the house. No one answered. But when she went to look out the window after the call Dan's car was gone. Chase had taken the car and the body of baby boy David which he brought back to his apartment. He parked Dan's car at the Sandpiper Apartment block and walked back home.

After several calls Neone and Tracy walked over to the Miroth house and rang the doorbell. They was no response. They tried the door. It was locked. Tracy looked in the window but couldn't see anyone. They decided to walk back to their own house. Neone spoke with another neighbor, Nancy Turner, and expressed her concerns. Nancy decided to check out the house. She tried the front door, and then went around to the back with her son.

The door was open so she went inside. She walked through the hall and into the kitchen and then turned to walk into the bedroom where she saw the mutilated body of Evelyn Miroth. The sheer graphic nature of the scene shocked her so much that she walked out and all she said to Neone was: "It's Evelyn and I think she's hurt and there's blood all over."

She then said they should call the police. At 12:43 p.m. Deputy Ivan Clark of the Sacramento County Sheriff's department arrived and spoke with Nancy Turner. Clark had, just four days earlier, witnessed the horrific injuries in the Wallin case but that experience didn't prepare him for what he saw now. He sealed off the house as a scene of crime area and called for back-up.

Detective Fred Homen was the first to respond. He noted that the Miroth landline was continuously ringing so eventually he answered it. It was Karen Ferreira. Another investigator told Karen that her sister-in-law was dead and two other people, a male adult and an older child were also dead. When she enquired about David she was told that he wasn't in the house. Later, Karen and her husband Tony arrived at the scene at approximately 3:55 p.m.

The following morning Rick Chase walked down to his local shop and bought a copy of the *Sacramento Bee* newspaper. The front page and several inside pages extensively covered the deaths in 3207 Merrywood in graphic detail with accompanying photographs. It brought a smile to his face and a thrill to his heart.

And, he still had the body of the infant David. Evelyn's older son, Vernon, was at school at the time of the murders, and her daughter, Lori, was living with her father and ex-husband, Vernon Miroth.

Mr. Miroth would arrive at his ex-wife's residence at about the same time the Sheriff's deputies and homicide investigators were racing to the scene. He was there to pick up Vernon Jr, who hadn't arrived home from school.

There can be no doubt that Chase knew what he was doing (he had planned the murders); that what he was doing was wrong (his attempts to conceal his involvement); and, that he took steps to avoid getting caught (wearing rubber gloves and hiding Dan's car). So, accordingly, on the face of it, he was legally sane. But this didn't mean he was mentally stable.

The massacre provided more information for the FBI profilers. His actions suggested an oblivious, unhinged mind and offered more information for refining the profile. Ressler and Vorpagel were sure he lived close to both scenes and ordered a massive local manhunt.

Police were looking for a tall, thin, white male with scruffy long hair who lived near the scene of the crimes. Unfortunately, there were many young men who fitted that description, although none as strange as Richard Trenton Chase. They began house to house enquiries as crime scene investigators examined the evidence.

They had found bloody prints in the house and it was likely that tests would inevitably lead them closer to their man. While the neighborhood was awash with crime scene investigator vans, print and media journalists, Rick, oblivious to the commotion, was at home mutilating the body of David Ferreira.

He cut off his head, drank his blood and ate some of his brain. His apartment looked like a nineteenth century abattoir with blood splattered over the floors, walls, ceiling and covering everything utensil and piece of furniture in the place.

The smell of putrefied rotting flesh was overwhelming. Luckily, for Chase, he never had visitors so no one was ever inside his apartment. But on that day when someone knocked on his door his heart skipped several beats.

It was a routine enquiry, part of the house to house investigation. He then made up his mind he had to dispose of the body immediately. He had escaped, for now. But very shortly he became a suspect and police were dispatched to interview him at his apartment.

When he was arrested outside his apartment he was carrying a large "MacFries" box and walking towards his car. The box contained bloody rags and papers, brain matter in an envelope, and David Ferreira's diaper pin. He also had Dan Meredith's wallet, driving license and credit cards in his back pocket. Police then checked out his apartment.

As investigators entered the apartment their senses were assailed by the overwhelming smell of blood. Blood was everywhere. In the bedroom they found a bloody plate on the bed, along with an adult's bloodstained clothing.

Three brain particles from David Ferreira were also sitting on the bed and feces was sitting on the bedroom floor. The walls were adorned with posters of internal human organs. In the kitchen they found a bloodstained hatchet, and in a bedroom drawer a bloody machete. There was a large bloodstain in the middle of the kitchen floor. When they opened the freezer they found a half gallon container of animal meat consisting of "kidney, liver or heart." Chase (pictured below) had a lot of explaining to do.

Initially, Chase refused to answer any questions other than a few he felt like answering. They tried the usual tactics: good cop-bad cop; the overwhelming evidence bit, "we know you did it, we have the evidence, just tell us why?; and the silent treatment where they just stared at him. Nothing worked. But at 7:00 p.m. he suddenly decided to talk. He signed a waver stating he understood his rights and was willing to speak with the investigators. That first night, at least four detectives, in two shifts, questioned him about the crimes, the Griffin, Wallin and Miroth homicides.

Despite the overwhelming evidence, he denied any knowledge of the murders and claimed that all he was guilty of was killing dogs. The more they questioned him, the more they realized how abnormal he was. Vorpagel faced this man down in the interrogation room, and Chase admitted he had committed the murders, but had done nothing wrong.

He was saving his own life, because his blood was turning to sand and he needed theirs to prevent it. Talking to someone like Chase helped to confirm what the profilers thought, and it was cases such as this that gave Ressler an idea about the prison interviews.

Over a dozen medical experts examined him looking for signs of insanity. There was no evidence of a compulsion to kill. He liked blood and thought it was therapeutic. One expert said he was not schizophrenic but suffered from an antisocial personality. His thought processes were working normally and he was aware of what he had done and knew that it was wrong. He was legally sane.

The trial began on the 2 January 1979. On the 8 May 1979, the jury, having found Chase to be sane at the time of the crimes, took less than five hours to decide his fate, guilty on all six counts. He was sentenced to death. He was dispatched to Cell 2N, on Death Row, in San Quentin, to await execution. The appeal process in California is so slow that many condemned prisoners actually die of old age before being executed. This was not going to be Richard Chase's fate.

On the 26 December, 1980, a prison guard, Officer Graham, checking cells found Chase lying awkwardly on his bed. When he opened the cell door and checked he found that the prisoner had stopped breathing. An autopsy determined that he committed suicide with an overdose of prison doctor-prescribed drugs called Sinequan, which are antidepressants, that he had collected over several weeks presumably for the very purpose of committing suicide.

The case was seen as another triumph for the FBI profiling methods. There was evidence that Chase intended to kill many more victims. He was on a learning curve. The success enjoyed by Ressler and Vorpagel was followed by John E. Douglas in the Francine Elveson murder case the following year. But then there was the "BTK" case.

## THE DENNIS RADER "BTK" CASE

Dennis Rader (pictured below) was a happily married man with two children. In fact, he was married for thirty four years and lived in the same house all his married life. His wife, Paula, worked as a book-keeper and sang in the Church Choir. Dennis was a doting husband who was never in trouble in his life. An ex US Navy man, he was gainfully employed. He was a Cub Scout leader. He was president of the congregation of his local Christ Lutheran Church.

He was also a psychopathic serial killer who liked to be called the *BTK Strangler*. BTK stands for Blind, Kill, Torture which is what Rader did between 1974 and 1991 in and around Kansas to at least seven women, one man and two children while masturbating over their bodies.

Dennis Lynn Rader was born on the 9 March 1945 to William Elvin Radar and Dorothea Mae (nee Cook) in Pittsburg Kansas. He was the eldest of four sons. He and his brothers Jeff, Paul and Bill were raised in the Park City area of Wichita, Kansas. His father, William was an ex-Marine. Dennis was baptized at the Zion Lutheran Church in Pittsburg, Kansas. He attended local schools and later graduated from Heights High School in Wichita in 1963. He attended Butler County Community College in El

Dorado, earning an associate degree in electronics in 1973. He earned a degree in the Administration of Justice from Wichita State University in 1979.

He married his wife Paula E. Dietz on the 22 May 1971. Paula was born on the 5 May, 1948 in Park City. Paula graduated from Wichita Heights High School in 1966. They had two children, Brian and Kerri. Brian Howard Rader was born on the 27 July, 1975 and joined the Navy in 2004. Kerri Lynn Rader was born on the 13 June, 1978. She later married Darian Rawson and moved to Farmington, Michigan in August, 2003. His wife, Paula, sang in the church choir and worked as a bookkeeper at Snacks, the Diamond Shamrock convenience store located at 61st Street North and Broadway.

Soon after they married they bought as their family home 6220 Independence, Park City, Kansas. It was a ranch-style, 960 square foot, three bedroomed house. Paula sold the house to Park City in January 2007. It was demolished in March 2007 to make access to a city park easier.

As a family man, Rader was known to be a strict disciplinarian. He had a tight Christian control over his family. He has been variously described as arrogant, rude, confrontational, meticulous, neat, efficient, friendly, a regular guy, and petty. He held a variety of jobs. He was in the US Air Force between 1965 and 1969. After this he joined the meat department in Leeker's IGA in Park City, and was an assembler at Colemans, a camping gear plant up until 1973. Between 1974 and 1988 he was a home security company called ADT Security Systems in Wichita, Kansas. Thereafter until his arrest he was a compliance supervisor for Park City.

After his arrest Paula Rader was described as being in a state of shock and disbelief and feeling bewildered and confused. She and her daughter Kerri went into seclusion in Michigan while his son Brian was said to be under a suicide watch. Paula claimed that she had no idea that her husband was a serial killer, despite living with him for thirty four years.

She obtained an emergency divorce from him soon after he was arrested. Based on testimony that her thirty four year marriage to Rader endangered her mental and physical health, the usual sixty day waiting period was waived for Paula. Rader did not contest the divorce or appear in court. He simply signed over all the couple's property and all of his retirement benefits. The marriage ended on the 26 July 2005.

Once arrested on the 25 February 2005 neither his wife nor their children ever communicated with him again except by letter in relation to the divorce. They did not attend the trial. An article by Jeff Chu in *Time* Magazine, on the 14 March, 2005 quoted Brent Lathrop, a long term friend of Paula Rader and later her boss at the Snack convenience store as follows:

> **Paula had been envied by women at her church for the way her husband doted on her, helping with her coat and always opening the car door. The possibility that her husband of thirty four years might be BTK has left her 'in quite a lot of shock.'**

Some commentators have questioned if Paula Rader knew of her husband's dark secret. She told police she knew nothing of his activities. But she did find a draft of a poem on a chair that was written in her husband's handwriting which described a brutal murder. That poem later appeared prominently in newspaper reports about BTK after a brutal murder. She knew he had boxes of papers stored in his closet. It was a small house. Did she ever check out those boxes?

Rader said he convinced his scared wife that the poem was written for a college class assignment when he was attending Wichita State University and taking classes in the administration of justice. Perhaps she was scared of her husband. The fact that in 1979 she saw him dressed as a woman and pretending to hang himself does not prove that she knew he was a serial killer.

Rader's *modus operandi* was to cut the external telephone lines of the victim's house, break into the house or con his way in, tie up the victims, slowly strangle them and watch them die. He would then masturbate over the body. He was methodical in his approach but less competent in its execution. He would stalk a victim for weeks before making an approach.

His murder campaign began on the 15 January 1974 when early in the morning between 7:00 and 7:30 he broke into the home of Joseph and Julie Otero at 803 North Edgemoor Street, Wichita. He had first cut the phone lines that morning and waited at the back door. He had been watching Julie Otero and her eleven year old daughter Josie for weeks. He liked Latina women: "I guess they just turn me on," he once told Ray Lundin, senior special agent for the Kansas Bureau of Investigation.

He timed it so that only Mrs. Otero and her daughter would be there but when he saw nine year old Joseph Otero Jr. open the back door to let the dog out he almost aborted the plan. His intention was to tie up and torture the two females and release his sexual fantasy. He decided to proceed and entered through the back door brandishing a gun. He was further surprised to encounter her husband and panicked and lost control of his intended plan. He told them that he was wanted by the police and needed food and a car. Mr. Otero offered him a car.

Suddenly, he realized he hadn't masked his identity and that they would now be able to recognize him. He decided to kill them or to use his own words "put them down." Rader had come equipped to blind, torture and kill just two of them and had packed the pocket of his Air Force parka with binding material and weapons. He began by putting a plastic bag over Joseph Otero's head.

He tightened it with cords which he had brought with him. But Joseph Otero was not the easy target he had expected. An airman himself and former boxer he tried to chew through the plastic bag meant to suffocate him. So Rader put another couple of bags and some clothing over his head and tightened the cords.

After that, Rader said he "worked pretty quick." He then strangled Mrs. Otereo: "After that I did Mrs. Otero... I had never strangled anyone before, so I really didn't know how much pressure you have to put on a person or how long it would take..." In fact, although Mrs. Otero had passed out she was still alive. In his confession Rader went on:

> **I strangled Josephine and she passed out... I thought she was dead and then I went over and put a bag on Jr.' s head and then if I remember right, Mrs. Otero came back... she came back, and... She was pretty upset with what was going on...I went back and strangled her again, it finally killed her at that time.**

But before Rader strangled Mrs. Otero again, she pleaded with him to save her son.

He then put another bag over Joey's head and took him into the other bedroom and put a cloth over his head, a T-shirt and bag so he couldn't tear a hole in it. He went out and got a chair so he could watch the nine year old boy struggle and finally die.

He then went back to Josephine who had woken up. She cried "What have you done to my Momma?" She then started crying: "Momma, Momma, Momma" and Rader mocked her by imitating her voice.

He then carried her to the basement. He put a rope around her head and tied her to an overhead pipe so that her toes could barely touch the ground. Rader later told police:

> **So my encore was to just take her down there and hang her. If she had been dead, I would have still hung her, just to hang her.**

He then pulled down her panties to her ankles and watched her slowly die while masturbating over her body. Rader told Josie:

> **Well, honey, you're going to be in heaven tonight with the rest of your family.**

After this he went through the house cleaning it up and took Mr. Otero's watch and a radio. Finally, after he had cleaned up, Rader took the Otero's car and parked it at a local shop called Dillons and walked back to his own car.

Rader did not kill again until the 4 April 1974. His next victim was twenty one year old Kathryn Bright. She was just one of a number of targets or "projects" as Rader called them that he had selected:

> **I was just driving by one day and saw her go into the house with somebody else and I thought that was a possibility, there was many places in the area, College Hill, they are all over Wichita, but anyway, it was just basically a selection process, work toward it, if it didn't work, I just move on to something else. But in my kind of person, stalking and trolling, you go through the trolling stage and then stalking stage. She was in the stalking stage when this happened.**

He broke into the house at 3217 East 13 Street by punching through the screen. He didn't know she had a brother called Kevin. He waited for her to come home. When she returned with her brother he pulled a gun on them and told them he was on the run and needed a car.

He knew that he would have to get the nineteen year old Kevin out of the way if he was to fulfil his sexual fantasy with Kathryn. He made him tie her up first and tied him to the bedpost. He brought her to another room where he tied her up again, this time to a chair.

When he went back to strangle Kevin he saw that the youth had loosened some of his bonds. He began fighting with Rader so Rader drew his gun and shot him. Assuming he was dead he went back to the sister to strangle her.

But he had also failed to tie her up properly and she also began to struggle. Just when he thought he had subdued her he heard a noise from Kevin's bedroom and went back in. Kevin was still alive so he tried to strangle him again and yet again Kevin fought him so Rader shot him a second time.

Finally subdued he went back to Kathryn and finding it impossible to strangle her he stabbed her several times in the ribs. After he was finished he heard Kevin escaping:

> **All of a sudden the front door of the house was open and he was gone, and oh, I tell you what I thought: I thought the police were coming at that time, that was it. I stepped out there; I could see him running down the street, so I quickly cleaned up everything that I could and left.**

When asked, at the trial, by Judge Waller if, on this occasion, he had brought a mask to hide his identity, Rader said he hadn't. Rader had clearly intended to kill her. Despite being shot twice Kevin survived. Unfortunately his sister Kathryn, although still alive when police got to the house, died later in hospital from her wounds. Thirty years later, police would find the knife Rader used to kill Kathryn Bright, a Boy Scout knife he kept in his kitchen pantry.

Apparently, Rader did not kill anyone else in the next three years. Between 1974 and 1977 his son Brian was born and he had a full time secure job at ADT Security Systems. So, why then, on the 17 March 1977 did he decide to kill again?

At his trial Rader said about the selection of Shirley Vian Relford:

> **It was completely random. There was actually someone across from Dillons that was a potential target. It was called project Green, I think...That particular day I drove over to Dillons and parked in the parking lot and watched this particular residence and then got out of the car and walked over to it. I knocked and no one answered it.**

Rader said he was "all keyed up" so he walked around the neighborhood until he met a young boy, Shirley Relford's son, and passing himself off as a private detective, asked him to identify some photos, which were actually of his own wife and son. Then Rader went to another address, knocked on the door, but nobody answered, so he went to the house where the boy went.

Twenty four year old Shirley Vian Relford answered the door of her house at 1311 South Hydraulic Street, Wichita. Rader described himself as a private detective and began showing her some photographs. He then produced a gun and forced his way into the house. Shirley who was in her nightgown and had three children in the house was terrified. He explained to her that he had a problem with sexual fantasies and was going to tie her up and maybe her kids too:

> **I explained that I had done this before and at that point in time, I think she was sick. She had her night robe on. If I can remember right, she had been sick and I think she came out of the bedroom when I went in the house. So we went to back to her bedroom and I proceeded to tie the kids up. They started crying and got real upset. So I knew this was not going to work. So we moved them to the bathroom, she helped me, and I tied the doors shut.**
>
> **We put some toys and blankets, odds and ends, in there for the kids, make them as comfortable as we could. We tied one of the bathroom doors shut so they couldn't open it, and she went back and helped me shove the bed against the other bathroom door. I proceeded to tie her up.**
>
> **She got sick, threw up. I got her a glass of water, comforted her a little bit and then went ahead and tied her up and put a bag over her head and strangled her. I had tied her legs to the bedpost and worked my way up and what I had left over [rope] and I think I looped it over her neck.**

Because he was having problems with the children, one escaped, Rader didn't have time to carry out his sex fantasy in its entirety. But he had time to put Shirley on her bed, tape her feet and ankles, and tie her up with her arms crossed under the small of her back. Her put a plastic bag over her head and tied it with a pink nightgown. On his way out he stole her panties so he could wear them later on in the comfort of his own home.

Before leaving he assembled his "hit kit" consisting of tape, cords and other items back into his briefcase, put them in his car and walked back to his car which he had parked in the parking lot of his local store, Dillons. Although one of the children, six year old Steven, gave a detailed description of the attacker, no one connected it to Rader. Dennis Rader, the *BTK Strangler*, had now claimed his sixth victim.

Ten months later Rader turned his attention to twenty five year old Nancy Fox of 843 South Pershing Street, Wichita. He told police it was his most satisfying kill of all. He had been watching her for some time:

> **I did a little homework. I dropped by once to check her mailbox, to see**

> **what her name was. Found out where she worked, stopped by there once, Helzbergs. Sized her up. The more I knew about a person, the more I felt comfortable. So I did that a couple of times. Then, I just selected a night, which was this particular night, to try it and it worked out.**

The night he chose to break into her home was Thursday the 8 December 1977. He knew what time she usually came home at so he cut the phone lines, broke in the back and waited for her in the kitchen. When she arrived home he confronted her and told her he had a sexual problem; that he would have to tie her up and have sex with her.

Nancy gave him the impression that she accepted her fate, smoked a cigarette and then went into the bathroom to undress. When she came out he handcuffed her, made her lie on the bed and tied her feet. He then got on top of her and strangled her with a belt. She struggled, called his fantasy “ridiculous” and clawed at his testicles which regrettably only spurred him on.

She fell into unconsciousness and he waited until she came round again before repeating the process. As she died he whispered into her ear that he was BTK. After he strangled her he took the belt off and retied that with panty hose.

He then masturbated over her body. When he was finished he took some personal items including panties and cleaned up any evidence he might have left. He left, walked to his car, several blocks away and drove home to his wife and young son. Having killed his victims Rader would fantasize about what place they would hold in his afterlife. Nancy Fox was to be his primary mistress.

Dennis Rader retired from serial killing in 1977 but for some inexplicable reason he re-commenced eight years later on the 27 April 1985 when he abducted fifty three year old Marine Hedge from her home at 6254 North Independence Street, Park City and strangled her to death.

Did he stop killing between 1977 and 1985? We don’t know. If he did stop, why did he start again? Again, we don’t know.

Marine was a neighbor who lived six doors away from the Rader family. She was a casual acquaintance to whom he would say hello as he walked by her house. Rader was excited at the prospect of killing someone who lived so close. On the night of her murder, he quietly broke into her house and waited in a closet for her to return. When she came home, she had a man with her who stayed about an hour. Rader:

> **I waited until the wee hours of the morning and then proceeded to sneak into her bedroom and flip the lights on real quick like, I think the bathroom lights. I didn't want to flip her lights on. She screamed.**
>
> **I jumped on the bed and strangled her manually. After that, since I was still in the sexual fantasy, I went ahead and stripped her. I am not sure if I tied her up at that point in time, but she was nude. I put her on a blanket, went through her purse, and personal items in the house. I figured out how I was going to get her out of there. Eventually, I moved her to the trunk of the car, the trunk of her car, and took the car over to Christ Lutheran Church, this was the older church, and took some pictures of her...in different forms of bondage and that is what probably got me in trouble is the bondage thing. But anyway then I moved her back out to her car.**

Unlike the other victims Rader choked her with his bare hands. He dumped her body in a culvert, used for dumping the carcasses of dogs, around 53rd between Webb and Greenwich where he covered her with trees and bushes. Initially, he thought about bringing her to a barn but took her instead to the Church.

He had already purchased plastic sheets and had hidden them so he could tape them over the windows. He laid her body on the altar and took pictures of her, tied up and in sexually graphic positions. Once again he was never suspected for this crime.

Twenty eight year old Vicki Wegerle was another of Rader's so called "projects." She loved to play the piano, and Rader heard the music when he would stalk her. She was playing the piano on Tuesday the 16 September 1986 when Rader called to her home at 2404 West 13th Street North, Wichita.

Posing as a telephone repair man from Southwestern Bell he talked his way into letting him into her house. He referred to the uniform as his "hit clothes" and told the court:

> **Basically things I would need to get rid of later. Not the same kind of clothes I had on. I don't know what better word to use, crime clothes, I just call them hit clothes.**
>
> **I walked from my car as a telephone repairman. As I walked there, I donned a telephone helmet, I had a briefcase, I went to one other**

> **address just to kind of size up the house. I had walked by it a couple of times, but I wanted to size it up more.**
>
> **As I approached it, I could hear a piano sound and I went to this other door and knocked on it and told them that we were recently working on telephone repairs in the area. Went to hers, knocked on the door, asked her if I could come check her telephone lines inside.**
>
> **I went over and found out where the telephone was and simulated that I was checking the telephone. I had a make-believe instrument. And after she was looking away, I drew a pistol on her.**

Rader instructed her to go into the bedroom so he could tie her up. She asked about her two year old son. He said he wasn't interested in the kid, only her. He used some fabric from her bedroom to tie her hands. But the fabric became loose and she tried to fight him off.

She put up a brave fight and scratched him so badly that she managed to get his DNA under her nails. He then grabbed one of her stockings and strangled her into submission. She begged him to stop and prayed as he killed her. When he thought she was dead, he rearranged her clothes and took several photos of her.

But he made a hasty retreat when he thought he heard her husband returning home. She was fatally injured from the strangling but was not yet dead when Rader left her home. Rader said he would see Vicki Wegerle after he dies "as one of the bondage slave women." In 2004 the DNA would be tested and positively identify Rader as her attacker.

He didn't kill for another five years and then on the 19 January 1991 Rader abducted sixty two year old Dolores "Dee" Davis, from her home on 117th Street North and North Meridian Street, Sedgwick.

On the day in question Rader used his position as a scout leader for an alibi for this murder. He told his wife he was helping to set up a January camp at Harvey County Park West. Afterwards, he parked his car at the Baptist church at 61st Street North near his Park City home. He dressed in dark clothes and assembled his "hit kit" of tape and restraints inside the Church. He walked nearly two miles across a field and a cemetery to get to the victim's house.

It was a secluded area. After she retired he threw a brick through a window and gained entry. She came out of her bedroom thinking that a car had hit her house only to be confronted by Rader. She pleaded with him not to hurt her. He told her he needed food and a car. He handcuffed her and checked on the car and pretended to prepare some food.

He then removed the handcuffs, tied her up and strangled her. He searched the house for some personal effects and panties to take as trophies. He put her in a blanket and dragged her to the trunk of her car and put her in the boot. He drove off in her car and realizing that he had forgotten his gun returned to the house to retrieve it. He then walked back to his car, picked up the victim's body and dumped it under a bridge.

There are a number of interesting facts about the Dennis Rader case. One is the length of time between the killings.

Another is that despite the fact that evidence of his killings could be found in his small family home, his wife never suspected her husband. He was married for thirty four years and didn't fool around, at least not with other women. But he did like to wear other women's underwear. He also liked to torture his victims and watch them die slowly.

He didn't care who he killed, men, women or children. He didn't have sex with any of his victims but liked to masturbate over them as their life drained away from their bodies. He would never have been caught if he hadn't boasted about his crimes to the police and media. Various profiles about him throughout the years never succeeded in capturing him.

For example, in 1997, Robert Ressler, helped outline a profile of BTK. Ressler thought the offender was probably a graduate student or a professor in the criminal justice field at WSU in Kansas, was most likely in his mid-to-late-twenties at the time of the killings. He felt he was an avid reader of books and newspaper stories concerning serial murders. Additionally, because his pattern of killings has not been seen in Wichita since the 1970s, Ressler believed:

> **He has left the area, died or is in a mental institution or prison. I've learned that if man gets the opportunity, he will do devious things. He has a dark side, whether it's poisoning his neighbor's roses or killing his neighbor.**

FBI Profiler John Douglas in the book *Obsession* stated that there were no defensive wounds found on any of the victims, assuming that the killer used a gun to control them. He further stated that the letters written by the killer and sent to the police had so much detail that he was convinced that the perpetrator had taken his own crime scene photos in order to have a keepsake of the crime to fantasize about later.

Douglas wrote that the killer used police lingo in his letters. He thought the killer could actually have been a police officer, or may have impersonated a police officer. He concluded that the killer probably read detective magazines and may have even have bought a police badge.

He attempted to insert himself in the investigation. He was tempted to brag or leave hints about what he had done.

Douglas was of the opinion that the killer was in all probability a loner, inadequate, in his twenties or thirties and might have had arrest records for break-ins or voyeurism, but probably none for actual rapes. He thought that the killer may have stopped killing because he was in jail for something else, or a mental hospital, or may have died, or may have injected himself so closely into the investigation, that he became frightened and distanced himself from the inquiry.

In August 2000, investigators contacted Dr. Deborah Schurman-Kauflin, President of the Violent Crimes Institute, and asked her to draw up a profile of the killer based on the information at hand. This is her profile:

> **From the information provided to me which is limited (no crimes scene photos, police report, etc), I have constructed the most likely type of person to have committed the murders in the 1970s. I do not believe the murders from the 1980s were connected.**
>
> **1. Single, white male 28-30**
>
> **2. Resided near Otters or spent time in the area to form fantasy about Josephine (this was his main target). Lived in a house, not apartment.**
>
> **3. Over 6'1, tall and trim. Neat in appearance with short hair. Clothes darker by choice.**
>
> **4. Considered quiet and conservative by those who would know him. Modest. I believe people would mistake him as kind because of his quiet demeanor. But he suffers from extreme pathology -- psychopath.**
>
> **There are no voices or demons. This man knew exactly what he was doing.**
>
> **He was and, if alive, still would be an extremely sad individual. Sad for himself and his pain. Completely self-absorbed.**

**Because I did not have access to the letters, his job status is questionable to me. I do feel that his job was very secondary to him. Money was not important either. His compulsion to kill was and ALWAYS would be number 1. He would not be satisfied with fantasy. He would be forced to act. Therefore, I find it hard to believe that he did not kill between 1974 and 1977. If there were no murders in Kansas at that time, he was someplace else.**

**He was very immature, the games, magazines, choice of child target. The fact that he did not sexually assault lends credence to this. He masturbated on the victims but did not rape.**

**At the same time, he is very patient in his crimes, stalking and killing without detection. This makes him a paradox, which in and of itself would be disturbing even to him.**

**I do feel like he is very comfortable with books and would have many of them in his home. Not just a few, many, many books. True crime as well as books, which feed his fantasies. I feel as if they would be found all over his house. He was smart, highly intelligent.**

**This is not someone who is heavily into drugs/alcohol. They do not cause his crimes. He may drink at times, but that would not be an excuse for the murders.**

**5. He had a car, which would have been dark in color as well. However, this is a person who would enjoy walking around neighborhoods looking at people and victims.**

**6. Due to his immaturity, he would be comfortable with people much younger than him. He would not have many friends, only acquaintances who really do not know him. All of his relationships would be superficial. He would not be married, and any history with women would be short-lived and meaningless.**

**This is not a person who would stop killing on his own. There are 3 reasons to stop:**
**1. Death**
**2. Prison**
**3. Too disabled or sick to kill**

**Period. This is a compulsive psychopath who enjoyed killing and wouldn't give it up. I generally give more detailed analyses but due to limited information, this is what I can provide.**

Unfortunately, the profile didn't help in any meaningful way. Although police invested 100,000 hours in at least a half-dozen investigations from

1974 until 1991, Rader was not caught. Eventually, the search for the *BTK Strangler* was scaled down to just one detective. It had involved thousands of suspects and cost hundreds of thousands of dollars in man-hours.

Then suddenly in March 2004, after so many years, the investigation was re-launched after someone sent a letter to *The Wichita Eagle* that claimed responsibility for the 1986 murder of Vicki Wegerle. The writer provided some very convincing evidence of the letter's authenticity by including crime scene photos as well as Vicki Wegerle's driver's license. The return address on the letter was from "Bill Thomas Killman" (BTK), 1684 South Oldmanor. The name and address were found to be fictitious. Later the police confirmed that the letter was from BTK. They said that the single fingerprint removed from the letter would most likely come back to an employee from the newspaper and not from the killer.

On the 25 March, 2004, former FBI profiler Gregg McCrary, (pictured above) gave an interview to *The Wichita Eagle* claiming the unsub was bragging about his kills because he craved the media attention:

> **Look at what I've done. He can't resist doing that. Frightening the public is like playing God. It's a heady, intoxicating experience, so they're not afraid to make contact with you (the media) or police; that's all a part of the game for a guy like this. He's outwitted law enforcement and everybody else all these years.**

On the 28 March, Psychologist Dr. Harold Brodsky told KAKE-TV that giving BTK attention was a good thing:

> **Are we falling into his hands by showing him this attention? The reality is, if we don't show him this attention, he's going to do something diabolical.**

On the 5 May, 2004, another letter suspected to be from BTK was sent to Kansas television station KAKE-TV. The letter was three pages long. On the first page was typed The BTK Story, under which was a list of chapters taken from Court TV's *Crime Library* story on the killer. The writer amended some of the chapter titles. For example, Chapter 7 originally titled BTK- The Next Step was changed to PJ's; Chapter 4 titled BTK- Different Worlds Collide was altered to read Fantasy World and the chapter titled BTK Cold Case Squad was altered to Will There (Be) More?

The second page of the letter was entitled Chapter 8 and contained word puzzles with letters in vertical rows.

The third page contained photocopies of business identity cards belonging to two men. According to an article in *The Wichita Eagle* one of the men was later contacted but could not understand why a photocopy of his ID was in the letter.

Curiously, the three page letter was different from the March letter sent to *The Wichita Eagle* in that the return address on the envelope bore the name Thomas B. King (TBK) instead of Bill Thomas Killman (BTK).

The FBI authenticated the letter as a genuine BTK communication, believed to have been his third in a three-month period. There was no doubt that the killer was back to his old habit of taunting police. But why? Maybe he missed the media attention he so craved? Or, maybe it was a warning of his intention to strike again?

On the 17 June, 2004 another letter was found in a mechanical engineering book in the drop box of the Wichita Public Library. The letter was yet another genuine BTK communication.

This time the letter detailed, *inter alia*, some of the events surrounding the 1974 Otero murders. It also include a poem he had written for one of his victims, Nancy Fox, who he killed in December 1977. Investigators failed to find any hidden meanings in the poem that might help them apprehend the killer. Investigators believed that BKT was trying to demonstrate that he was much smarter than those trying to catch him. On that score he was right, for now.

That Fall a British film crew travelled to Wichita to make a documentary on BKT. The party included a British psychic named Dennis McKenzie. McKenzie had successfully assisted in several high profile investigations, including the Soham murders.

He said he was able to contribute to the BTK investigation by producing an image of the killer with the help of a sketch artist, as well as other potentially valuable information concerning the murder cases. Nothing fruitful came from it all.

On the 24 October, 2004, the 30th anniversary of BTK's first communication with the authorities, another letter from BKT was left at a UPS drop box outside the OmniCenter building at 250 N. Kansas Street in Wichita, Kansas.

In the meantime, the authorities continued to pour over clues left by BTK. It was clear he had gone to great efforts to misguide and confuse the authorities by providing them with false information mixed with subtle truths.

They now believed he was highly educated or at least well read in that he was familiar with the works of James Joyce and Native American writer Thomas King. They began to wonder if he studied literature at Kansas State University.

In November 2004, police publicly disclosed for the first time information that BTK revealed about himself in a letter. The personal information was released in the hopes that someone might recognize the killer's description and come forward with even more information about his identity or whereabouts.

Jeanene Kiesling of KAKE-TV gave out these new details on the 30 November, 2004:

BTK claims he was born in 1939, which would make him 64 or 65 years old.

His father died in World War II. His mother and grandparents raised him. He has a fascination with railroads and between 1950 to 1955, his mother dated a detective with the railroad.

In the early 1950s he built and operated a ham radio. He also has knowledge of photography and can develop and print pictures.

He also likes to hunt, fish and camp.

In 1960, BTK claims he went to tech school and then joined the military for active duty and was discharged in 1966 at which time he says he moved back in with his mother.

He worked repairing copiers and business equipment.

He admits to soliciting prostitutes.

The problem was that no one really knew if this information was accurate or provided to throw investigators off the scent. Most serial killers are pathological liars. Why would BKT be any different?

Suddenly, at around 7:30 p.m. on the 1 December 2004, prompted by an anonymous tip-off, police arrested a sixty four year old man at his south Wichita home.

The media reported that the arrest was connected to the BTK case. Initially, investigators denied that the man arrested was in any way linked to the murder investigation. But on the 26 February 2005, after thirty one years, the identity of Wichita, Kansas' most notorious serial killer, known as BTK, was made public.

Dennis L. Rader, 59, of Park City, Kansas was taken into custody after having been stopped at a traffic light near his home on East Kechi Road shortly after noon that day.

There is conflict as to whether or not his daughter Kerri (pictured below) now called Kerri Rawson, provided a DNA sample to help determine his guilt. He was formally charged on the 28 February with ten counts of first degree murder and pleaded not guilty.

On the 27 June during a court hearing he unexpectedly made a full and frank confession and pleaded guilty. He was sentenced to ten consecutive life terms without a chance of parole. Because Kansas had no death penalty at the time the murders were committed, life imprisonment was the maximum penalty allowed by law.

He is serving his sentence at El Dorado Correctional Facility in Kansas. He is confined to the cell twenty three hours a day with the exception of voluntary solo one-hour exercise yard time. He has access to a shower three times a week. His earliest possible release date is the 26 February, 2180. A family member of one of his victims described him as human skin covering a black cancerous hole.

The failure of profilers to help assist in his capture was seen as a major set back by critics of the profiling approach. If nothing else the case proved that criminal profiling had its limitations and despite its recent success the approach was fallible. And then there was the case of Gary Ridgway.

## THE GARY RIDGWAY CASE

The 15 August 1982 is a day Robert Ainsworth is unlikely to forget. On his descent down the Green River towards the outer edge of Seattle's city limits forty one year old Ainsworth noticed what he thought was a mannequin floating in the water. In an attempt to snag it with a pole he accidentally overturned his raft and fell into the river. As he did he realized to his horror that the eyes peering up at him were not those of a mannequin at all. They belonged to a dead black woman.

In a matter of moments he noticed a second dead body of a semi-nude black woman floating beside him which was partially submerged under water. He swam ashore to seek help and eventually did, half an hour later, when a father and his two children were cycling through the area. Shortly afterwards, the police arrived, cordoned off the area and began to search the river and surrounding area.

It wasn't long before they found a third body, that of a young girl partially clothed. But this body was not submerged in water. It lay approximately thirty feet away in a grassy area from where the other bodies were. The victim appeared to have died from asphyxiation.

She had a pair of blue pants knotted around her neck. Bruising on her arms and legs indicated that she had put up a struggle. She was later identified as sixteen year old Opal Mills who had been murdered within twenty four hours of discovery.

The Chief Medical Examiner Donald Reay examined the bodies at the scene and determined that all three girls died from strangulation. The two girls found in the water were later identified as thirty one year old Marcia Chapman and seventeen year old Cynthia Hinds.

He also discovered that the bodies in the water had pyramid-shaped rocks lodged in their vaginal cavities and were tied down by rocks in the water. Chapman, a mother of two, had been dead for over a week and Hinds for just a few days.

But it wasn't just three dead bodies.

Several days earlier, the nude body of Deborah Bonner was found slumped over a log in the Green River. Her cause of death was also strangulation.

And a month before that, the body of Wendy Lee Coffield was found strangled and floating in the Green River.

Moreover, six months prior to her discovery, the body of her friend Leanne Wilcox was found several miles from the river in an empty lot. Originally, investigators did not believe that killer they called the *Green River Killer* had murdered Wilcox, but now they had an open mind. Six months, six bodies, all found in or near the Green River. There was only one logical conclusion, there was a serial killer on the loose.

*The Seattle Times* advised the increasingly worried citizens that the largest police task force since the Bundy murders a decade previous was to be assembled and led by Major Richard Kraske, the head of the Criminal Investigation Division and Detective Dave Reichert of the King County Major Crime Squad. They were soon joined by the FBI serial killer profiler

John Douglas. It was a formidable team. But it was still hopelessly undermanned.

Within weeks they found themselves swamped by a deluge of leads from the public. The result was that, just as in the English case of the *Yorkshire Ripper*, Peter Sutcliffe, much of the data and information they received was lost, misfiled or completely overlooked. But what they did discover was that many of the victims were involved in prostitution and knew each other.

Police concentrated their search in the main red light district of Seattle which stretched from South 139th Street to South 272nd Street. Investigators interviewed hundreds of prostitutes in an effort to gather information on any suspicious characters they might have encountered. But many of the girls refused to co-operate and progress was slow.

However, a lead did emerge when one girl who worked the area filed a report stating that she had been raped by a man who had made a reference to the Green River murders.

Hopes were raised when on the 28 August 1982 police announced that they had a suspect in custody but because they could not find any plausible evidence to link him to the murders he was released without charge. Two other prostitutes filed reports claiming that a man driving a blue and white truck had abducted them and tried to kill them.

One report was filed by 21 year old Susan Widmark who claimed that she had been abducted by a middle-aged white man who violently raped her in his truck on a desolate road while holding a gun to her head. He had spoken about the Green River murders. She managed to escape from the truck and record part of the registration number before he sped away.

A second witness, Debra Estes, who was just fifteen, claimed that she had also been forced to give a man in a blue and white truck, oral sex while he threatened her with a gun. Her assailant had released her in the woods. An APB was sent out to find the truck and driver. And then, a month later, they had a break.

Charles Clinton Clark was a meat butcher who was pulled over by the police while cruising the red light district in his blue and white truck. Police discovered he owned two handguns. Widmark and Estes both positively identified him as their assailant. Following interrogation he admitted to their assaults. But, was he the serial killer?

During the time many of the Green River victims disappeared Clark was able to provide the police with a solid alibi. Moreover, while he was being charged with the rape of Widmark and Estes a nineteen year old woman, Mary Meehan, disappeared while out walking near the Western Six Hotel situated smack bang in the middle of the red light area. But why would a serial sex killer be interested in an eight month pregnant woman?

Because of the volume of information being received the investigators were obliged to seek help from public volunteers. One such volunteer was a forty four year old unemployed cab driver. The cab driver came under suspicion due mainly to an old fashioned hunch of Detective Reichert.

The hunch was based on a profile of the killer as devised by FBI agent John Douglas and the fact that two weeks prior to Meehan's disappearance, two sixteen year-old girls, Kase Ann Lee and Terri Rene Milligan, mysteriously disappeared.

Douglas (pictured above) believed the *Green River Killer* was a confident, yet impulsive middle-aged man who would most likely frequent the murder scenes, in order to re-enact the crimes in his mind. He would have been familiar with the area and was likely to be deeply religious.

The cab driver fitted the profile and soon became the prime suspect. He also knew five of the victims. Having nothing to connect him to the killings police initially arrested him for unpaid parking fines.

Meanwhile, on the 26 September police discovered the body of seventeen year old Gisele A. Lovvorn. She had gone missing two months earlier. Her decomposing naked body was discovered by a biker near abandoned houses south of the Sea-Tac International Airport. She had been strangled to death with a pair of men's black socks.

What was interesting about the case was that, at the time of her disappearance, she was blonde, but when her body was discovered her hair had been dyed black.

The Task Force investigation began to flounder and between September 1982 and April 1983, approximately fourteen other girls disappeared including Mary Meehan, Debra Estes, Denise Bush, Shawnda Summers, Shirley Sherrill, Rebecca Marrero, Colleen Brockman, Alma Smith, Delores Williams, Gail Matthews, Andrea Childers, Sandra Gabbert, Kimi-Kai Pitsor and Marie Malvar. They ranged in age from fifteen to twenty three years and all worked as prostitutes. And then they lucked out.

Marie Malvar's boyfriend told the investigators that the last time he saw her was on the 30 April 1983 when he saw her get into a dark colored truck as she solicited on the street. Watching from a distance he thought that Marie and the driver had argued over something so he decided to follow the truck as it sped away. Unfortunately, he lost them at a light. He never saw Marie alive again but as luck would have it, less than a week after the incident, he, along with Malvar's father and brother, spotted the suspicious truck near the place where he initially lost sight of it days earlier.

They followed the truck to a house located on South 348th Street and called the police. The police arrived and questioned the owner of the truck. Gary Ridgway denied having ever seen Marie Malvar and accordingly the police did not pursue the matter any further.

Around the same time, Kimi Kai Pitsor's pimp saw her getting into a dark green pick-up truck with a driver he described as having a pockmarked face. He watched as the two drove off and he never saw Pitsor again. He filed a report with the police but no connection was ever made between the two reports.

Although they didn't have sufficient evidence to charge him, the cab driving volunteer was their prime suspect and they continued to keep him under investigation. In reality, the Task Force was getting nowhere.

They decided to enlist the help of renowned criminal investigator Bob

Keppel. Keppel compiled an analysis of the Task Force for the sheriff of King County, Vern Thomas, which was highly critical of the on-going investigation. All the data needed to be re-categorized to ascertain common threads. As the authorities argued over what to do and the cost of doing it more bodies were discovered.

On the 8 May, the remains of twenty one year old Carol Ann Christensen were found by a family hunting for mushrooms in a wooded area near Maple Valley. Her killer had taken the trouble to display her corpse in an unusually gruesome way. Her head was covered by a brown paper bag.

When the bag was removed they found that she had a fish carefully placed on top of her neck. Another fish was placed on her left breast and a bottle between her legs. Her hands were placed crossed over her stomach. Freshly ground beef was placed on top of her left hand.

Further examination revealed that the victim had been strangled and her body had spent some time submerged in water. But, what could the experts make of the killer's motivation by the way he had left the body? In a word, nothing.

Between the spring and summer of 1983 Martina Authorlee, Cheryl Lee Wims, Yvonne Antosh, Carrie Rois, Constance Naon, Tammie Liles, Keli McGuiness, Tina Thompson, and April Buttram all disappeared. They were all aged between fifteen and twenty one and most were involved in prostitution.

In June, the unidentified remains, which were believed to be of a seventeen to nineteen year-old white woman were found on SW Tualatin Road.

In August, the body of missing Shawnda Summers was discovered near the Sea-Tac Airport. One day later the remains of another body, which remained unidentified, was found at the Sea-Tac Airport North site. The fall and winter of 1983 would also yield as many disappearances and even more corpses.

In fact, between September and December of 1983, nine more women went missing and seven bodies were discovered, all of whom were believed to have been abducted and murdered by the *Green River Killer.* The missing women, who were mostly prostitutes, included Debbie Abernathy, Tracy Ann Winston, Patricia Osborn, Maureen Feeney, Mary Sue Bello, Pammy Avent, Delise Plager, Kim Nelson, and Lisa Lorraine Yates. Those whose bodies were discovered included Delores Williams, who had gone missing in March 1983.

Her remains, and those of Gail Matthews were discovered on the 18 September at Star Lake.

Over the next few months, the bodies of five more women were discovered. The skeletal remains of Yvonne Antosh, who was last seen on the 31 May, were found near Soos Creek on Auburn-Black Diamond Road on the 15 September. Twelve days later, the partially buried skeleton of Constance Naon was found in an area south of Sea-Tac Airport.

The Task Force conducted a search of the area where the bodies were found and discovered another body, that of twenty two year old Kelly Ware.

Yet more bodies were discovered, those of Mary Meehan and the skull of Kimi-Kai Pitsor. Two weeks later the Green River Task Force was increased by more than half. They feared that many more murders would occur in the coming months. They were right. It was becoming crystal clear that had the victims not been prostitutes much more would have been done by the authorities much earlier.

Changes were necessary. They soon came.

In January 1984, Captain Frank Adamson of the Police Internal Affairs Unit was appointed to head up the Green River Task Force. He took immediate action beginning with the re-location of the task force HQ to the Burien County precinct, an area near where the crimes were occurring.

He also divided up various tasks and assigned them to individuals within the team. He then assigned three detectives to a newly-constructed crime analysis section, whose duties involved the follow-up of leads and analysis of possible trends and methodologies utilized by the killer, as well as other pertinent information relevant to the case.

The focus was changed from investigating a suspect's possible guilt to the suspect's possible innocence. This strategy allowed investigators to quickly eliminate people under suspicion who had alibis and instead concentrate on more probable suspects.

The remaining suspects were then prioritized according to their threat. Category "A" was for those who were most closely linked to victims and fitted the profile of the killer and his movements.

Those who were less closely linked with the crimes were assigned to categories "B" or "C" before being eventually eliminated. The net was closing in on the Green River Serial Killer, but not nearly fast enough.

On the 14 February 1984, the body of Denise Louise Plager was discovered forty miles from the city close to Interstate 90. Nine more bodies would be discovered over the next two months; all were linked to prostitution. A profile of the killer was emerging:

- His targets were young prostitutes.
- He had several dumping grounds.
- He disposed of the bodies of his victims.
- Most were discovered partially buried or covered with garbage or foliage.
- Most had been found off isolated roads or near illegal waste dumping areas. The FBI's profiler John Douglas concluded that the bodies were dumped in the areas because the killer thought of the women as "human garbage."

In April 1984 shoe impressions indicated the killer was a size 10 or 11. It was a vital clue that would later prove decisive. But still they were no nearer to catching the killer. And then a strange thing happened.

Barbara Kubik-Pattern was a psychic working as a volunteer task force operative. In the middle of April she claimed to have had a vision that a woman's body would be found close to Interstate 90. She immediately contacted the police but when they failed to act she took it upon herself to investigate.

She soon discovered another body. Immediately after the discovery, Barbara and her daughter drove to a nearby search area that was patrolled by the police. When she informed one of the officers of her discovery, she was rebuffed and even threatened with arrest for obstruction of the guarded perimeter. But later they believed her and were confronted with the gruesome discovery. The media had a field day.

But this victim did not fit the usual victim's profile. Amina Agisheff was a thirty six year old mother of two who worked as a waitress. She was last seen on the 7 July, 1982 walking home from her work at a restaurant in downtown Seattle.

In May the skeletal remains of fifteen year old runaway Colleen Brockman were discovered by two children. Three years had passed and the killing spree had continued unabated.

And then the most unlikely savior appeared in the form of the infamous serial killer Ted Bundy. From his prison cell on death row, Bundy offered to assist Keppel and the task force in finding their man. He told Keppel he would help him get into the mind of the killer. It was an offer Keppel couldn't refuse.

Bundy (pictured above) suggested that the killer knew his victims, probably even befriending them before he lured them to their deaths. According to Keppel's book *The Riverman*, Bundy believed the killer most likely disposed of even more bodies where they found the more recent ones. Moreover, he believed the disposal pattern of the bodies led closer to the killer's home.

There was nothing new in this information but Bundy was able to give unusual insight from a killer's prospective, which did ultimately prove valuable.

The total body count had climbed to thirty one, although only twenty eight of the victims actually made it on the ever-growing "official" Green River murder list. Fourteen women were still believed to be missing.

Meanwhile, FBI profiler John Douglas re-evaluated the previous profile of the killer and came to a new conclusion. Douglas now believed that due to the extent of the body count there had to be two separate killers.

Douglas suggested that, although the profiles of both killers were similar in many ways, the way in which they disposed of the bodies slightly differed. Although the theory was plausible there were still no suspects to support it. Skeletal remains continued to be discovered. Was there no end to the killing? But then, eventually, the Task Force had a breakthrough.

In February 1986, a man described by investigators as a "person of interest" was brought in for questioning. Media speculation mounted. But once again the suspect was released without charge.

The Task Force was now being portrayed as incompetent, an expensive joke. Except, there was nothing funny about their incompetence. The number of victims was quickly climbing toward a staggering forty. The cost was becoming prohibitive.

Consequently, the staff was reduced by 40% and Adamson was reassigned to another project. Captain James Pompey became the new leader of the Green River Task Force.

Pompey immediately began to reorganize the team and the data related to the investigation. Just as Pompey was beginning to get started, two more bodies were discovered in December. This time the bodies were found much further away than expected in an area north of Vancouver, British Columbia.

Yet again, the killer seemed to be taunting investigators. Even more intriguing was the fact that the partial remains of several other women had been scattered alongside the bodies of the two women. Despite the fact that the bodies were located a great distance from the others, there was no doubt in the investigators' minds that the work was that of the *Green River Killer.*

Investigators now had a new suspect in relation to the Green River murders. He was previously known to police. He had been picked up for attempting to solicit an undercover police officer posing as a prostitute. However, after he successfully passed a lie detector test they were obliged to release him.

But when they delved deeper into his past, they discovered that he had been accused of choking a prostitute in 1980 near the Sea-Tac International

Airport. Yet, the man pleaded self-defense after claiming the woman bit him and he was soon after released from police custody.

But Detective Matt Haney had lingering doubts over the innocence of this suspect. He began digging into his history a little deeper. He discovered he had previously been stopped and questioned in 1982 while he was in his truck with a prostitute.

The investigator learned that the prostitute he was with was Keli McGinness. Keli was one of the women on the Green River murder list. The following year the same man was questioned in connection with the kidnapping of murder victim Marie Malvar. Yes, Haney believed he had a strong lead. But, was he right?

Haney questioned the suspect's ex-wife and discovered that he often frequented the dumpsites where many of the bodies had been discovered. He also matched the description provided by several prostitutes as a regular cruiser of the red light district between 1982 and 1983. He claimed that his work obliged him to pass through this area on a daily basis.

The suspect was a truck painter. Most damaging of all for him was that he was found to have been absent or off duty on every occasion a victim disappeared. The suspect was Gary Ridgway (pictured below).

On the morning of the 8 April, 1987, the police obtained a warrant and searched the man's house. But, they found nothing incriminating and Ridgway was released without charge. Meanwhile, Captain Pompey died from a massive heart attack related to a scuba-diving accident and was replaced by Captain Greg Boyle. More dead bodies were discovered. Their deaths were attributed to the *Green River Killer.* Although there were still bodies being discovered, there were no recent killings. Had he stopped killing? Or maybe he had just moved on?

In 1988, the discovery of more than twenty bodies of prostitutes in San Diego led to the belief that the *Green River Killer* had moved on and was now continuing his murderous rampage in California.

Detective Reichert and the new task force commander Bob Evans temporarily joined forces with the San Diego police department in an effort to find the killer. And then a new suspect emerged at the end of December 1988.

William J. Stevens was a student in the School of Pharmacology at the University of Washington. But he was something else as well.

During an airing of the popular true crime detective show Crime Stoppers several callers phoned him in as a potential suspect. It appeared that he was a prison escapee who was on the run for eight years, after a two-year stint behind bars for burglary.

In fact, he had been a suspect already in the Green River murders. Associates told police that Stevens had a pathological hatred of prostitutes and had often spoken about killing them. Despite intense interrogation and an exhaustive search of his home and that of his father police found nothing to link him to any of the killings. Eventually, Stevens was cleared of all involvement in the Green River murders.

The skeletal remains of two more young female victims were discovered in October 1989. One of those was Andrea Childers whose body was found in a vacant lot near Star Lake and 55th Ave. South. However, due to the state of decomposition of her body the police were unable to say for certain how she had died.

In early February 1990, the skull of Denise Bush was found in a wooded area in Southgate Park in Tukwila, Washington. The remainder of Bush's body had been discovered in Oregon five years earlier.

The investigators were now convinced that the killer was deliberately moving body parts around in an effort to confuse them. If that was his intention, then it was working. Not only were they confused, they were demoralized. By July 1991 the once formidable Task Force was reduced to just a single investigator named Tom Jensen.

Headlines said it all, "Nine years, Forty Nine victims, $15 million, No clues". The investigation became known as America's largest unsolved murder case. The file on the *Green River Killer* was to remain dormant for ten years.

Gary Leon Ridgway was born in Salt Lake City, Utah, to Mary Rita Steinman and Thomas Newton Ridgway on the 18 February 1949. He had two brothers, Gregory Leon and Thomas Edward. He suffered a troubled childhood with a domineering mother and a set of parents who constantly argued.

As a child he would wet his bed. His mother would immediately bathe him but at the same time belittle and embarrass him in front of the family. Gary had conflicting feelings of sexual attraction and anger towards her. He had a low IQ and performed below par at Tyee High School, at one point having to repeat a year just to pass. Class mates described him as congenial and forgettable.

At the age of sixteen Ridgway led a six-year-old boy into the woods where he attacked him with a knife, stabbing him through the ribs into his liver. According to the victim and Ridgway himself, Ridgway walked away laughing and saying, "I always wondered what it would be like to kill someone." After graduating from High School he married nineteen year old Claudia Barrows, a school girlfriend. But with a poor education and little prospects he decided to join the navy and was dispatched to Vietnam, where he served on board a supply ship and saw combat.

It was during his time in the military that Ridgway developed an appetite for prostitutes. His insistence on having unprotected sex resulted in him contracting gonorrhea. The disease so angered him that he developed an intense hatred for all prostitutes.

Meanwhile, back home, his wife Claudia, alone and bored, engaged in an extramarital affair. The marriage broke up and ended within a year. He later remarried a girl called Marcia Winslow but this second marriage also ended in divorce due largely to infidelity.

It was during this second marriage that Ridgway found religion. In fact, he became so religious that he began proselytizing door-to-door, reading the Bible aloud at work and at home, and insisting that Marcia follow the strict teachings of their church pastor. He was also known to frequently cry after sermons or reading the Bible.

But when he wasn't reading the bible he was having sex with as many prostitutes as he could afford. He became so obsessed with sex that he often requested his second wife to participate in sex in inappropriate places. Sometimes he wanted sex in areas where his victim's bodies were later to be discovered.

Like the *Yorkshire Ripper*, Peter Sutcliffe and *Boston Strangler*, Albert De Salvo, Gary Ridgway had an insatiable sexual appetite. He would regularly demand sex several times a day and often in public places or in the woods.

Outwardly, he hated prostitutes and frequently complained about their presence in his neighborhood, but he also took regular advantage of their services. Psychologically, Ridgway was torn between his staunch religious beliefs and his uncontrollable lusts. In 1975, his second wife gave birth to Ridgway's son, Matthew. Ridgway kept a photograph of Matthew in his wallet.

In April 2001 Detective Reichert (pictured below) was now the sheriff of King County. It was twenty years since the start of the Green River killings but Reichert believed that now, with the advent of DNA, that it was time to re-examine the cases. He began by forming a new task force team initially consisting of six members.

The task force included DNA and forensic experts and a couple of detectives. But soon the force grew to more than thirty. All the evidence from the murder examination was re-examined and some of the forensic samples were sent to the labs. Finally, they were making progress.

The first samples to be sent to the lab were found with three victims that were murdered between 1982 and 1983, Opal Mills, Marcia Chapman and Carol Christensen. The samples consisted of semen supposedly taken from the killer. The semen samples underwent a newly-developed DNA testing method and were compared with samples taken from Ridgway in April 1987. Result!

On the 10 September 2001, Sheriff Reichert broke down in tears on receiving news from the labs that a match had been made between the semen samples taken from the victims and Gary Ridgway.

But it was not until the end of November that Ridgway was intercepted by investigators on his way home from work and arrested on four counts for the aggravated murder of Mills, Chapman, Christensen and Cynthia Hinds.

At the time of his arrest Ridgway was working for a computer company. At the time of the murders, he was employed as a truck painter for thirty years at the Kentworth truck factory in Renton, Washington. He owned many trucks during that time.

Three more victims, Wendy Coffield, Debra Bonner, and Debra Estes, were added to the indictment after a forensic scientist identified microscopic spray paint spheres as a specific brand and composition of paint used at the Kenworth factory.

On the 5 November 2003, Ridgway entered a guilty plea to forty eight charges of aggravated first degree murder as part of a plea bargain organized by his counsel, Anthony Savage.

He agreed that in return for a life sentence he would co-operate in locating the remains of his victims and providing other details. In his statement accompanying the guilty plea, Ridgway explained that all of his victims had been killed inside King County, Washington, and that he had transported and dumped the remains of the two women near Portland to confuse the police.

At the trial, the deputy prosecutor, Jeffrey Baird told the court that the deal contained "the names of 41 victims who would not be the subject of State v. Ridgway if it were not for the plea agreement."

Due to sustained public unrest King County Prosecuting Attorney Norm Maleng was obliged to explain his decision to make the deal:

> **We could have gone forward with seven counts, but that is all we could have ever hoped to solve. At the end of that trial, whatever the outcome, there would have been lingering doubts about the rest of these crimes.**
>
> **This agreement was the avenue to the truth. And in the end, the search for the truth is still why we have a criminal justice system ... Gary Ridgway does not deserve our mercy. He does not deserve to live. The mercy provided by today's resolution is directed not at Ridgway, but toward the families who have suffered so much.**

On the 18 December 2003, King County Superior Court Judge Richard Jones sentenced Ridgway to forty eight life sentences with no possibility of parole and one life sentence, to be served consecutively.

He was also sentenced to an additional ten years for tampering with evidence for each of the forty eight victims, adding four hundred and eighty years to his forty eight life sentences.

Ridgway's notoriety lies in the fact that he confessed to more confirmed murders than any other American serial killer. In February 2004, county prosecutors began to release the videotape records of Ridgway's confessions.

In one taped interview, he told investigators initially that he was responsible for the deaths of sixty five women, but in another taped interview with Reichert in December 2003, Ridgway claimed to have murdered seventy one victims and confessed to having had sex with them before killing them, a detail which he did not reveal until after his sentencing.

In his confession, he said that he had sex with his victims' bodies after he murdered them, but claimed he began burying the later victims so that he could resist the urge to commit necrophilia.

Ridgway talked to and tried to make his victims comfortable before he committed the murders:

> **I would talk to her... and get her mind off of the, sex, anything she was nervous about. And think, you know, she thinks, 'Oh, this guy cares'... which I didn't. I just want to, uh, get her in the vehicle and eventually kill her.**

Ridgway was a typical psychopath who forgot his victims, had a "hard time keeping them straight," never learned their names, and wrote them off as vicarious thrills. To him they were all simply disposables or throwaways:

> **I killed some of them outside. I remember leaving each woman's body in the place where she was found. I killed most of them in my house near Military Road, and I killed a lot of them in my truck not far from where I picked them up.**

He claimed that they were all killed in King County, hoping that prosecutors outside King County would believe him and not prosecute him. His contempt for women in general and prostitutes in particular was evident in his plea bargain statement:

> **I picked prostitutes as my victims because I hate most prostitutes and I did not want to pay them for sex. I also picked prostitutes as victims because they were easy to pick up without being noticed.**
>
> **I knew they would not be reported missing right away and might never be reported missing. I picked prostitutes because I thought I could kill as many of them as I wanted without getting caught.**

Ridgway exhibited typical serial killer behavior when he expressed his interest in reliving the murder experience. This provided him with a sense of empowerment, something he lacked in his everyday life. He buried his victims in clusters so that he could drive by and remember the cluster and the pleasure he experienced in the murder of those victims.

King County officials were anxious to create the impression that the plea bargain brought closure to this case. But, does it?

Was Ridgway a killing machine solely in the years between 1982 and 1984? Did he suddenly stop until he murdered once more in 1990 and then once again in 1998? Perhaps, but such a pattern is not typical of what usually happens in the macabre world of the serial killer, particularly serial sex killers.

Speculation is rife that Ridgway killed many more victims and buried them outside of King County. It took many years to find the bodies that were part of this plea bargain. It may take many more years to find the rest of them. Somehow it's hard to accept that we finally have closure in the case of the Green River killings.

Wilson, Lincoln, and Kocsis (1997) indicated that in respect of the above three case studies the profiles for Richard Trenton Chase was accurate and the case was solved; the profile of Gary Ridgway was inaccurate and the profile did not lead to the arrest of the suspect; and in the Dennis Rader case the profile was ambiguous and it did not lead to the arrest of the suspect.

They compared the results of twenty one cases altogether in their study including the Montana Murders, the Georgia Murders, the USS Iowa case, Richard Chase, Gary Ridgway, Wayne Williams, the Calabro Murder, the Soult Murder, the Devier Murder, the .22 Calibre Murders, the Fort Benning Killer, the Stocking Strangler, George Russell, the Prante Murder, the Bell Murders, the Shawcross Murders, Denis Rader, Robert Hansen and the 1-40 Killer. While the profile success rate was high it was by no means universally correct.

Today the FBI provide behavioral-based and operational support through the NCAVC's Behavioral Analysis Unit (National Centre for the Analysis of Violent Crime).

They assist law enforcement agencies mainly in America by reviewing and assessing the criminal act, by interpreting the offender's behavior during the crime, and the interactions between the offender and the victim during the commission of the crime and as expressed in the crime scene (FBI, 2008).

But does this approach to criminal profiling actually work?

## THE ORGANIZED DISORGANIZED TYPOLOGY

One of the more well-known examples of a classification system for offenders is that of the Organized Disorganized typology of serial killers outlined by Ressler, Burgess and Douglas (1988). The word's "organized non-social" and "disorganized asocial" first appeared in an article entitled The Lust Murderer in 1980 (Hazelwood & Douglas 1980).

Since then they have been cited in numerous textbooks on profiling and have caused much confusion and been the subject of criticism. Even the words "disorganized" and "organized" are considered a false dichotomy by some. It's now generally accepted that the terms were oversimplifications made for the benefit of law enforcement by FBI profilers.

In particular, they oversimplify the psychiatric terms "psychotic" and "psychopathic" which were intended to be psychiatric diagnoses. There are important differences between a psychotic individual with a diagnosable mental illness and a psychopathic individual (like a psychopath, sociopath, antisocial personality disorder) with only a character disorder.

These differences are inferred via inductive reasoning from crime scene characteristics. A "disorganized" that is a psychotic, mentally ill individual is inferred from a chaotic, disorganized crime scene where a lot of evidence is left behind.

An "organized" individual by which is meant a psychopathic who knows right from wrong but shows no remorse, is inferred from a controlled, well planned, and premeditated, organized crime scene where little evidence is left behind. But this, in itself, is an oversimplification as Owen (2004) and Petherick (2005) point out:

## DISORGANIZED

Victims of disorganized killers are often battered about the face or sometimes blindfolded, reflecting a need to depersonalize the victim, or because the victim might resemble someone in the killer's life for whom he feels fear or anger. Any sexually sadistic acts committed will usually be done after the victim is dead, and if the body is left at the crime scene, it will usually be in plain view, but some disorganized killers take the victim's remains with them as trophies.

Footprints, fingerprints, and sometimes even the weapon are found at the crime scene or discarded nearby. Often the crime scene itself will be chaotic and in total disarray. FBI research shows such killers are often below average in intelligence and socially inadequate. Within a family, they are usually among the younger children, with a father who combines harsh discipline with an unstable employment history.

The disorganized killer will himself have a poor employment record in an unskilled job, after possibly dropping out of school, and will tend to live on his own, or with an older family member, with minimal contact with people outside the family, and often tend to go out only after dark. They will have poor hygiene and low self-esteem, showing little to no interest in the news media, and will tend to live or work near the crime scene.

They will either have no personal transport, or the vehicle they have will be old and badly maintained. Because they commit crime under stress, this can trigger changes in behavior, such as increased use of drugs, alcohol, or a turn to religion. They often return to the scene of the crime and sometimes turn up at the victim's funeral or memorial service even occasionally placing "In Memoriam" messages in the local paper. Some keep a diary.

## ORGANIZED

In organized killings, there is likely to be signs of planning and care to avoid detection and identification. The location(s) where the victim is seized and taken will involve careful planning. Organized killers usually personify their victims, selecting them according to a preference by type, age, gender, appearance, occupation, lifestyle, and very well other details which would seem trivial to anyone else.

They will usually be socially confident enough to strike up a conversation, present themselves as non-threatening, and not appear odd or suspicious. He is usually above average height and weight, with impressive appearance and clothing. He uses his own vehicle or the victim's vehicle for transport. In many cases, the victim will be raped before, or even instead, of being killed.

Any weapon used will usually be taken away afterwards, as will any restraints such as chains, ropes, belts, gags, or blindfolds. The body too will often be taken away, to be disposed of carefully, making discovery less likely.

So, there are both similarities and differences. Both types of criminal may return to the scene of a crime; both tend to have few close friends although the organized offender is a loner by choice. This is because he feels as if he is better than others; is usually in stable long term skilled or semi-skilled employment; and is sexually competent and in a long term relationship.

Organized offenders usually have experimented with drugs and alcohol. They are likely to have their own transport which will be well-maintained and in good condition. They familiarize themselves with local media output on their crimes which assists them in monitoring police investigations. After committing a crime the organized offender may change employment or move house as a precaution against getting caught.

Because he is better educated and more confident it is easier for him to transplant himself.

As stated earlier the disorganized/organized approach has many critics and they point out the following weaknesses in the approach:

1. Most crime scenes have mixed characteristics displaying both disorganized and organized characteristics. However, the FBI point out that "mixed" ought to be reserved for cases where the crime has been interrupted;

2. The focus on the amount of evidence left behind tends to ignore the context of the situation;

3. The typology contains an inherent bias in favor of disorganized for crimes motivated by hate, anger or domestic violence as well as those committed by those under the influence of drugs or alcohol;

4. Psychotic is not the polar opposite of psychopathy;

5. The mental condition of a serial offender can deteriorate during the course of his killing spree as in the case of Ted Bundy, as well as improve over a criminal career. Accordingly, it is argued that the typology completely ignores such an evolution. (See what Canter says about this in the next section.)

6. Signature (the why) characteristics are overlooked in favor of *modus operandi* (the how) characteristics; and,

7. The typology presumes the ability to diagnose mental illness without the benefit of clinical intervention.

According to Holmes and De Burger (1988) the original profiling conducted by the FBI which was based on thirty six interviews was shaped by intuition, educated guesswork, and the agents' experience in criminal investigations. This begs the question: Is this a sufficiently scientific approach? Furthermore, the typologies were not quantitatively tested or based on stringent methodological research and other researchers have subsequently discovered deficiencies within the profiles produced (Alison and Canter, 1999; Muller, 2000).

Coleman and Norris (2000) found the organized disorganized dichotomy was based on a very small sample of interviewed sexual murderers and lacked any comparison or control group while Canter et al. (2004) point out that the interviews relied on retrospective self-reports from the offenders. These can be very inaccurate as they rely on the offender's memory about specific points in time and on 'trust' that the offender did not lie about their experiences and offences. More importantly, no comparison group was used. This calls into question whether any of the variables are actually specific to adulthood sexual murder perpetration.

As well, the majority of the sample used by Ressler, Burgess and Douglas did not experience social deviance in the early years of their lives. This has been frequently found in the backgrounds of sexual homicide perpetrators (Meloy, 2000). This means that any conclusion drawn using this dichotomy will not be generalizable across any other sample or study.

As stated above, the original sample of men were identified as either organized or disorganized not based on any scientific research or theoretical underpinning but on the combination of experience and intuition of the officers involved in conducting the study (Muller, 2000).

This intuitive separation was done *a priori*, before any statistical tests were used to analysis the differences between the two groups. Some critics (Kocsis, Irwin and Hayes, 1998) say that this was bound to lead to a self-fulfilling prophecy, rather than a valid behavioral dichotomy. And if you think about it, this is true.

Canter (1994) also criticized this classification on the basis that the boundaries between the two distinctive typologies of serial murders were often blurred and non-distinct. Canter believes that many offenders would be a hybrid of more than one type (Canter et al., 2004).

Keppel and Walter 1999 also argued that neither group is particularly rich in detail, nor does the typology address key issues relating to the offender's identity, nor lend to the apprehension of the offender as they often leave the investigator with some abstract notion of the offender and the crime.

In short, the inability to confidently and consistently assign offenders to one or the other type of offender affects the ability to draw concrete conclusions about the offender's characteristics, and in turn questions the pragmatic utility of this classification system.

To balance the argument it is important to point out that the approach has its supporters and most significantly, it is still in use today. Its supporters make the following points:

There is a long line of sociology and criminology, starting with pre-Shaw & McKay social disorganization ideas, continuing through the work of the so-called social pathologists, and most recently in the broken windows (decay, disorder, and incivilities) thesis of community policing that supports the making of inferences between disorganization of the scene (macro) and that of individuals (micro). It's all about context.

The more important part of the typology is to point to the degree of personality aberration, not the ability to "read" crime scenes and make medical diagnoses. Accordingly, supporters argue that whether the typology points to *modus operandi* or signature is irrelevant;

Waldo and Dinitz (1967) claim that there is sufficient evidence that criminologists have been making medical diagnoses for many years. Yablonsky (1966) for example, characterized the leaders of gangs as psychopaths without actually having met a gang leader while Sutherland (1937) drew careful generalizations about the psychology of all criminals from a sample size of one (Chic Conwell).

The whole thrust of criminological usage of terms like "psychopath" (McCord 1983) and related concepts of personality aberration is all about evolution (deterioration and improvement) of mental state. This is clearly evident in the Cambridge-Somerville and other cohort studies (McCord & McCord 1959).

However, whether you are a critic or supporter the fact remains that the organized disorganized dichotomy is not as significant or relevant today as it was a decade ago. Furthermore, the arguments against the validity of the organized disorganized typology greatly outweigh the support in its favor.

## THE HOLMES AND HOLMES TYPOLOGY

Another typology of serial murder was introduced by Holmes and Holmes (1998). In fact, it was a development of a previous typology of Holmes and De Burger, proposed ten years earlier.

Their typology outlined five classifications of serial murderers. It was produced through the examination of 110 known serial murderers, case studies, court transcripts, interview data, biographies and clinical reports. There are five types in their classification.

## VISIONARY KILLERS

Visionary killers are those who claim that voices tell them to kill. The *Yorkshire Ripper*, Peter Sutcliffe, claimed to hear voices in a graveyard he worked in. He would be regarded as a visionary killer. Visionary killers suffer from psychotic breaks from reality and believe that a higher power is commanding their actions.

For example, Albert Fish, *The Grey Man*, claimed to have had divine instructions to kill. Sometimes offenders may also claim that the crime was committed by another person in their body. Their crimes tend to be chaotic and disorganized.

## MISSION KILLERS

Mission killers murder those individuals they have judged as unworthy or undesirable. These killers believe they are getting rid of society's ills by eradicating a section of the public they believe are bad for society. Common examples are prostitutes, those of different races or religions and homosexuals. Their offences are swift, with no pre-mortem or post mortem activities. Gary Ridgway, *The Green River Killer*, is an example of a mission killer as he targeted prostitutes.

## HEDONISTIC THRILL AND LUST KILLERS

This group murder for the pleasure and excitement of the kill, which is often a long process. Whereas, the hedonistic-lust killer murders for sexual gratification, both when the victim is alive and after they have been killed. Both subtypes plan and organize their crimes. These killings focus on sexual gratification and sadistic acts. The amount of torture and the acts they perform on their victims add to their satisfaction.

Ted Bundy would be a prime example. Thrill killers get a "high" from the act of killing and getting away with it. Comfort killers usually kill for money and are more likely to kill people they know or family members.

## THE POWER CONTROL ORIENTED KILLER

The fifth type of killer, the power or control killer is motivated by the need for power and dominance over another person, and they gain greater gratification the longer the offence goes on (Canter & Wentink, 2004).

The primary motivation is domination; having and exerting total control over their victims. They use rape and murder as a method of exerting control. Despite the fact that they claim that each offender's behavior will have a dominate theme that would relate to their background characteristics and from this they would be able to be classified into a distinct category.

Canter and Wentink (2004) point out that Holmes and Holmes' types are not mutually exclusive. And while, the classification system may use different variables and words to describe the crimes and offenders, it is largely influenced by the original FBI organized disorganized typology (Canter, Alison, Alison, & Wentink, 2004).

Other critics include Hicks and Sales (2006) who have questioned the reliability and validity of the main types claiming that there is no indication of any theoretical or empirical derivation.

Canter and Wentink (2004) not only criticized the fact that the type were not mutually exclusive but outlined five major criticisms of the typology. The first relates to the conduct of the interviews. They say that there is a lack of any systematic account of how the interviews with 110 serial murders were conducted, and how these interviews led to their classification system.

Secondly, they argue that there was no direct empirical testing of the five typologies (until their own testing). Accordingly, there is no verification of co-occurrence of any type.

The terminology used to describe each typology is not properly described, that is, act-focused versus process-focused. This lack of proper description brings ambiguity as to under what conditions an offender or offence should be assigned to one type or another.

A further criticism was the overlap of features between the five typologies. For example, controlled crime scene, body movement, specific victim were listed for both lust and power control killers.

The fifth criticism concerns the inherent assumptions of a typology which Holmes and Holmes' typology fails to adhere to.

As Canter and Wentink write on page 493:

> **The inherent assumptions which Holmes an Holmes' typology fails to adhere to] with each type, the characteristics that define that specific type are likely to co-occur with one another with regularity...and specific characteristics of one type are assumed not to co-occur with any frequency with the specified characteristics of another type.**

Finally, when they tested the five types using a multidimensional approach they found little evidence to support the distinction between the serial murders based on Holmes and Holmes 1989 typology.

## THE KNIGHT AND PRENTKY MODEL

In 1990 Knight and Prentky produced a classification model of sexual offenders called the Massachusetts Treatment Center Rape Classification System (MTC:R3).

The model is primarily based on the motivation of the offender and takes into account that many offenders may not fit into a discreet number of limited categories.

It is based on the assumption that while sex offenders are a heterogeneous group, there will be some similarities in those offenders who commit sexual assaults (Knight, 1999; Robertiello & Terry, 2007).

Based on the examination of clinical and criminal files, self-report measures, standardized tests, and clinical interviews, the MTC: R3 includes four typologies.

## SEXUAL OFFENDERS

The sexual offenders are subdivided into non-sadistic offenders (those with low/high social competence) and the sadistic offender (those exhibiting fantasy/nonfantasy). Both types are preoccupied with sex and aggression, as well as physical inadequacy (Goodwill, Alison, & Beech, 2009; Robertiello & Terry, 2007).

## THE ANGRY OFFENDER

The pervasively angry offender, who are motivated by anger and hatred, and will use violence regardless of victim resistance; and the vindictive offender (with low/high social competence) motivated by power, control, and hatred, who are likely to physically harm, humiliate, and degrade their victims.

## THE OPPORTUNISTIC OFFENDER

The opportunistic offender (with low/high social competence) whose offences are impulsive and unplanned predatory acts, with immediate sexual gratification as the motivating factor.

Supporters claim that the MTC: R3 is a valid and reliable classification system for studying and classifying sexual offenders (Fargo, 2007; Knight, 1999), and a valuable framework in devising and providing treatment programs for offenders (Canter, Bennell, Alison, & Reddy, 2003; Knight, 1999).

Critics claim it is not without its potential limitations. Goodwill et al. (2009) claim that the interpretation and classification of the offender into one of the types in the MTC: R3 is partly subjective and based on the interpreter's experience, skill, and intuition, which potentially leads to more unreliability.

Barbaree et al. (1994) expressed concerns surrounding the generalizability to a wider population as the typologies were developed using only those offenders held within the MTC, which are a sample of "sexually dangerous" offenders and therefore not representative of other samples of sexual offenders.

## THE FBI CRIMINAL PROFILING PROCESS

Ressler et al. (1988) have outlined the six stages of generating a criminal profile used by the FBI.

### STAGE ONE

Stage one, profiling inputs, is about gathering and studying all the information that is relevant to solving the crime. This includes the crime scene information, victimology, forensic information, police reports, and forensic photography.

Any information that deals with possible suspects should not be examined or included; as such information may unconsciously prejudice the profile and distort the impartiality and objectivity of the profile.

### STAGE TWO

Stage two is the decision process models in which all the profiling inputs are organized and arranged into significant patterns.

It is during this stage that aspects of the type of homicide are evaluated, for example, whether it is a single, double, triple, mass, spree, serial killing.

They also consider the primary objective of the offender, for example whether the homicide was a primary or secondary motivation. They evaluate the victim risk level, their age, life style, and the risk of apprehension for the offender.

The levels of escalation, the amount of time for the committing of the crime and location factors are also assessed during this stage.

### STAGE THREE

Stage three is the crime assessment stage and involves the profiler reconstructing the sequences of events of the crime to establish just how certain things happened, how the people involved interacted with each other and to determine which category the crime fits into, that is, whether it is organized or disorganized.

The offender's motivation is considered at this stage and combined with the overall assessment of the crime scene.

### STAGE FOUR

The fourth stage is the generation of the criminal profile.

The background information, physical characteristics, habits, beliefs and values, and pre-offending behavior will be included and commented on based on the crime scene information provided. It is only at this stage that investigative recommendations might also be made.

**STAGE FIVE**

The fifth stage in profile generation is the application of the profile to the investigation.

The criminal profile is written into a report, provided to the agency and added into the investigation. The profiler will re-evaluate the profile if or when new information becomes available.

**STAGE SIX**

In the sixth and final stage, apprehension, the profile is evaluated for its accuracy and success at identifying the suspect.

Using this technique, expert crime scene interpretation is used to produce a profiling strategy based on profiling inputs which includes information collected by investigators such as;

- Complete photographs of the crime scene, including photographs of the victim in the case of murder;

- Any physical evidence;

- The autopsy report including pictures and any results of laboratory tests carried out on the victim;

- A complete incident report;

- Any police reports;

- Witness statements;

- An extensive background report on the victim to include; Occupation (former and present); Medical history, physical and mental; Address (former and present); Fears; Reputation, at work and in his/her neighborhood; Personal Habits; Physical description, including dress at the time of the incident; Social Habits; Information and background of victims family and parents, including victim's relationship with parents; Marital status, including children and close family members; Educational level; Use of alcohol and/or drugs; Financial status, past and present; Hobbies; Friends and enemies; Recent changes in lifestyle; and, finally, recent court actions.

After examining the evidence the profiler applies the rule known as "Ockhams Razor", a medieval rule, which states that "plurality should not be assumed without necessity" (translated in modern parlance to the KISS principle, Keep It Simple, Stupid). Or, as Sherlock Holmes would have said; "when you have eliminated the impossible, whatever remains, however improbable, must be the truth."

This wealth of detailed information is studied with a view to formulating the decision process. This involves organizing the input into meaningful questions such as;

1. What type of murder has been committed?. (mass murder, spree murder, serial murder)

2. What is the primary motive for the offence? (sexual, financial, personal, emotional disturbance)

3. What level of risk did the victim experience?

4. What level of risk did the murder take in killing the victim?

5. What was the sequence of acts before and after the killing?

6. How long did these acts take to commit?

7. Where was the crime committed?

8. Was the body moved?

9. Were the murder site and discovery site the same?

Using this information the profiler attempts to reconstruct the behavior of victim and killer.

Questions are asked to further categorize the offender, these might include;

a) Was the murder organized ?(suggesting a killer who carefully selects victims in order to act out a particular fantasy)

b) Was the murder disorganized? (suggesting a killer an impulsive, possibly psychotic killer).

c) Was the crime staged to mislead the police?

d) What motivations are revealed by details such as; cause of death; location of wounds; position of the body.

In the use of this model it is accepted, as a general rule, that brutal facial injuries point to a killer who knew their victim. Murders committed with any weapon that comes to hand reflects greater impulsiveness and the possibility that the killer lives close to the victim, whereas use of a gun as a murder weapon suggests less impulsiveness. It is also accepted that murders committed in the early morning do not usually involve alcohol or drugs.

The FBI admit that the profile is not a perfect tool and the information gleaned can vary from one profile to another but suggests that the information gathered in a profile may include; the offender's race; Sex; Age range; Marital status/domestic arrangements; General employment; Psychological characteristics, beliefs and values; Reaction to questioning by police; Degree of sexual maturity; Whether the individual might strike again; Criminal record checks including possibility of the commission of similar offences (Ault et al., 1980).

## LIMITATIONS OF THE CRIME SCENE ANALYSIS APPROACH

So, what of the validity of this approach? Although some FBI studies have included the statistical procedures and findings of their research (Ressler et al 1986; Hazelwood & Warren 1989) most of the published material does not.

It is often claimed that FBI profiling predictions have a success rate "in excess of 80 percent" (Canter and Heritage 1990; Blackburn 1993) but according to Pinizzotto (1984) the origin of this claim comes from a personal communication rather than any publicly documented study.

Pinizzotto's study is important because it is one of the few to provide analysis of the FBI profiling techniques. In a study of 192 requests for offender profiles, Pinizzotto found that 46% were deemed to be of benefit in the investigation but only 17% were of assistance in the actual identification of the suspect.

However, 77% of respondents claimed that the profiles did give a clearer focus for their investigation process thus reinforcing its use as a tool rather than a crime-solving technique.

Similarly, in Holland most police report benefit from the use of profiles (Jackson et al 1993). Over 97% reported that the profiles provided by the police intelligence service were useful. However, they did not produce any tangible link to the actual resolution of the crimes.

Later work by Pinizzotto and Finkel in 1990 compared profiles for homicide and sexual assault cases by professional profilers, detectives, psychologists and university students. Despite admitted defects in the case data, no significant differences were observed for the homicide case but the profilers were superior to the other groups in creating an accurate profile in the sexual assault case (Pinizzotto and Finkel 1990).

What this study demonstrates is that profiling works best where there is a wealth of information available for investigation and this is more likely to be found in a sexual assault case, where the victim, as a participant, is in a position to provide significant details of the attack and attacker.

The study also demonstrates that profilers have an enhanced ability to extract the most information from the least detail.

The FBI currently takes the lead in research on the development of criminal personality profiling. The value of the FBI's unit is often measured by the amount of resources allocated to it and its ever expanding nature (Van Zandt & Ether 1994).

The Association of Chief Police Officers in the United Kingdom, for example, now houses a specialized criminal personality profiling subdivision which parallels that of the FBI (Morley and Clark 1993).

But, while the FBI model of profiling still remains highly influential, another form of profiling emanating from Britain, and called investigative psychology (IP), pioneered by Professor David Canter is now beginning to rival and some argue, surpass, the FBI approach.

Some even suggest that it will, in time, become the only approach for criminal profiling.

# 4 INVESTIGATIVE PSYCHOLOGY

*He just waited until I stopped talking and said, 'Jesus, kid, you're almost a detective. All you need now is a gun, a gut, and three ex-wives. So what's your theory?*

**John Green, *Paper Towns* (2008)**

The Investigative Psychology approach otherwise known as the statistical-research approach to criminal profiling, pioneered by British psychologist Professor David Canter (pictured below) (e.g., Canter, Bennell, Alison, & Reddy 2003; Canter & Heritage, 1990; Canter, Hughes, & Kirby, 1998; Canter & Ioannou, 2004) claims to be grounded in scientific methodology and, according to Ainsworth (2001) is based on the multivariate analysis of the behavioral and other crime scene data to infer the characteristics, and psychological process of the unsub.

The predictions emanate from the analysis of the characteristics and crime scene information of offenders who have previously committed crimes and those who have been apprehended, and the contrast of these to those under investigation (Snook et al., 2008).

In establishing the field of Investigative Psychology, Canter emphasizes the reliance on psychological principles and strongly advocates the use of scientific methods such as falsifiability, transparent processes, and empirical-based theory in investigative focused research and its application, including criminal profiling.

No one can argue that the introduction of sound psychological principles to the detection and prevention of crime does not have its advantages but one has to wonder if the approach is too heavy handed to actually work in real life crime situations?

The answer is no and while the approach may not yet be foolproof it is clearly a step in the right direction in the fight against crime. In fact, the approach has already proved to be successful in fields beyond just criminal profiling.

Many commentators argue that had the approach, in its current form, been available and utilized at the time of the hunt for Britain's *Yorkshire Ripper* that the offender, Peter Sutcliffe, would have been captured years earlier.

The case of the British serial killer Peter Sutcliffe brought a general awareness of the problems facing law enforcement agents in tracking down random killers. Sutcliffe was the most notorious serial killer Britain ever had since the days of *Jack the Ripper.*

His first three attacks occurred in the second half of 1975. The first two victims were viciously assaulted while the third victim was knocked unconscious with a hammer and then stabbed to death.

She was the first of thirteen murders over the course of the following five years. Most of the women were prostitutes and were stabbed and slashed repeatedly in the stomach and vagina, although the killer stopped short of actually disemboweling them.

By early 1978, the hunt for the *Yorkshire Ripper* had become the biggest police operation ever mounted in Britain. They simply couldn't catch him. Their main problem was the vast number of suspects and leads to follow up.

Their search was akin to a needle in a haystack search. They had to manually follow thousands of leads on everything from suspects, tire marks, car number plates and a £5 note.

The suspect himself was interviewed several times but because of the sheer volume of information collected and not properly processed he evaded capture. All in all, 150,000 people were interviewed and 27,000 houses were searched. The result was that Sutcliffe was allowed continue his killing campaign. He was interviewed so many times that his fellow workers jokingly called him the Ripper.

After the thirteenth murder victim the police set up an advisory team of experts to study the murders all over again. For the first time they began to use a computer to estimate the "centre of gravity" of the murders. This led them to the conclusion that the killer lived in Bradford and not in Leeds, the city in which they were focusing enquiries.

They then decided to interview everyone again who lived in Bradford. This would have included Sutcliffe but as fate would have it he was caught before then, by sheer luck.

In May 1981 he was sentenced to life imprisonment and moved to Broadmoor, a secure hospital for the criminally insane. But the *Yorkshire Ripper* case taught the British police a valuable lesson. If suspects, like number plates, had been fed into a computer, Sutcliffe would probably have been caught three years earlier and three lives would have been saved.

Let's look at two case studies were aspects of investigative psychology were utilized in an attempt to capture the offender.

## THE JOHN DUFFY RAILWAY RAPIST CASE

In the next major investigation of a serial killer the British Surrey police began with a list of 4,900 possible suspects, all of whom were sex offenders. The list contained the man they were looking for.

The *Railway Rapist* began his campaign in 1982. At this stage two men were involved in raping five women at or near railway stations. By 1984 one of the men went solo. He threatened his victims with a knife, tied their hands and violently raped them. Between 1984 and 1985 there were twenty seven such attacks reported to the police.

In January 1986 the body of nineteen year old Alison Day was discovered in the River Lea. She had vanished seventeen days earlier. She had been raped and strangled.

Then four months later in April 1986, fifteen year old Dutch girl, Maartje Tamboezer, was attacked as she took a short cut through the woods near Horsley. She too was raped and strangled. But police noticed that her attacker was aware of recent advances in forensic detection and had taken precautions to evade capture.

He had stuffed a burning paper handkerchief into her vagina to prevent any "genetic fingerprinting." Her attacker had been seen running for a train shortly after the attack and subsequently two million rail tickets were examined in an attempt to find his fingerprints.

The following month, twenty nine year old secretary Anne Lock disappeared on her way home from work. Her body was not found for ten weeks.

Again the attacker had endeavored to destroy sperm traces by burning material inside her vagina.

At this stage those police forces involved in the investigation made a decision to pool their resources by linking their computers. The result was that the initial list of 4,900 sex offenders was now reduced to 1,999.

At number 1,594 was a man called John Duffy (pictured below). All the police knew about him was that he had been charged with raping his ex-wife and attacking her lover with a knife. But, significantly, the computers also showed that he had been arrested on suspicion of loitering near a railway station. Since the blood group of the killer of Anne Lock had been the same as the *Railway Rapist*, police had been keeping an eye on railway stations.

Duffy was called in for questioning. They noted the fact that he bore a similarity to the description of the *Railway Rapist* in that he was small, had ginger hair and his face was pockmarked. Nothing much came of the first interview but they decided to interview him again. Unfortunately, when they came to interview him he was in hospital suffering from amnesia. He claimed he had been severely beaten up by muggers. The medical staff at the hospital refused to allow him be interviewed. As he was just one of two thousand suspects the police dropped their interest in him.

What they didn't know was that John Francis Duffy and another man, David Mulcahy (pictured below), had been lifelong friends since their days together at school in north London. They both shared an early sadistic streak for tormenting and torturing animals starting with a hedgehog. Mulcahy had beaten it to death with a plank when he was just thirteen.

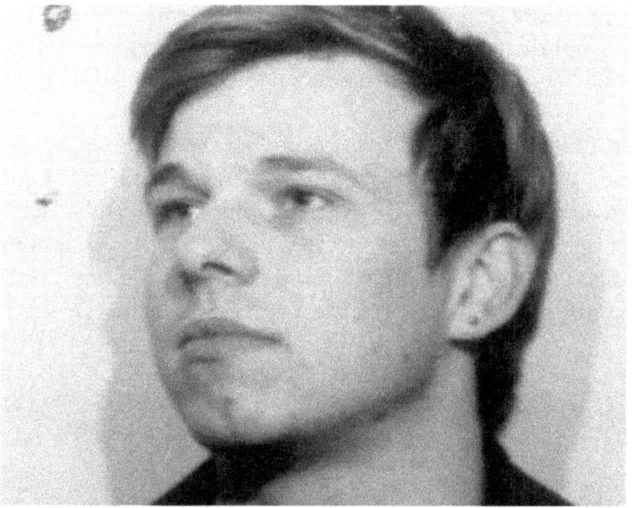

As they grew up the boys began to transfer their sadistic and misogynistic tendencies to women, each fuelling the other's dark sexual fantasies. Bullied at school, the two boys degenerated into a secret life of depravity, violence, rape, and murder. They developed a severely psychotic side to their personalities at an early age.

As he grew older, Duffy married and became a martial arts fanatic. Their brutal reign of terror began on the 1 July 1982, when the pair attacked and violently raped a twenty three year old woman in north London close to Hampstead Station.

Despite his previous convictions, Duffy was still able to carry out a string of sexual assaults and commit two murders over a fifteen month period. The Hampstead assault gave the two psychopaths a taste for terrorizing women in similar scenarios and for the next year they assaulted and raped women across London and its suburbs. All in all, eighteen women were raped near various train stations, as well as in an area close to Duffy's Kilburn house.

The police set up an urgent workshop to try to find the perpetrators, called Operation Hart. It was the largest investigation to take place in the U.K. since the *Yorkshire Ripper* investigation a few years earlier. In Autumn 1983 the attacks suddenly stopped. Police later found out that this coincided with Duffy's separation from his wife.

Early in 1984 the attacks began again, this time in west London and north London. The police had no evidence to link the crimes and were unsure as to whether they were committed by the same man, or two different individuals.

Then, in July 1985, three women were raped on the same night, all in the Hendon and Hampstead area. Duffy and Mulcahy were pulled in for interrogation, but were eventually released.

However, in August 1985, after a bout of domestic violence at his home, where he attacked his wife, Duffy was arrested. He was interviewed and eventually added to the Hart computer system as one of many thousands of men being investigated.

Unfortunately, Duffy was far down the list of suspects. Mulcahy, who was Duffy's accomplice in the rape attacks, was also questioned and eventually released.

At this point, the police called in the services of Dr. David Canter. Canter was a professor of psychology at the University of Surrey. They asked him to review the evidence.

Using techniques similar to those used by the *Yorkshire Ripper* team in studying the location of the attacks and the groundbreaking but seldom mentioned work carried out by Professor Stuart Kind, he concluded that the "centre of gravity" lay in the north London area and that the rapist probably lived within three miles of the Finchley Road.

Canter also believed that the rapist was a semi-skilled worked who was married but had a stormy relationship with his wife.

When Canter's analysis was matched up with the remaining suspects, the computer immediately spat out the name John Francis Duffy. Duffy lived in Kilburn in north London. Police initially decided not to arrest him but to keep him under surveillance. They continued to do this until another schoolgirl was violently raped and then arrested him.

Five rape victims picked him out at an identity parade. A search in the home of his parents uncovered string. The string was identical to that which had been used in the murder of Maartje Tamboezer. Forensic scientists also matched fibers from Alison Day's sheepskin coat to fibers found on one of Duffy's sweaters.

Professor David Canter had drawn up a list of seventeen personality and characteristic traits, including environmental clues, that the offender may display. When Duffy was finally caught, Canter was proved correct on at least twelve of these traits.

After the attack on the fourteen year old schoolgirl Duffy's luck began to run out. While stalking a woman in a park on the 7 November, he was discovered and arrested. The next day, Duffy was charged with three murders, and seven counts of rape.

Mulcahy was also arrested, but later released due to lack of evidence. It would be two years before Duffy would speak out and admit that he carried out the attacks with an accomplice.

Duffy went on trial in February 1988 and was convicted of two murders and four rapes, though he was acquitted of raping and killing Anne Locke. He was given a minimum sentence of thirty years by the judge, later extended to a whole life sentence by the Home Secretary.

This was rescinded by a European Court of Human Rights ruling, that later removed the right of politicians to reset sentence lengths.

Duffy kept silent about having an accomplice until he decided he wanted to clear his conscience while undertaking a counseling session. He chose not to reveal any more information about his partner in crime until nearly fifteen years later in 1997 when he implicated Mulcahy.

The police had suspected Mulcahy for years but had no evidence on which to convict him until Duffy's confession.

Duffy also admitted his involvement in the attack on Anne Locke, although he couldn't be retried under the double jeopardy rule.

However, Mulcahy, a married father of four had been tracked for several months by police prior to his arrest. DNA tests, which were not yet in use during the original investigation, finally proved his involvement conclusively.

In 2000, Duffy appeared in court as a witness against Mulcahy and gave detailed and graphic evidence over fourteen days. It was the first time a highest-category prisoner had ever given evidence against an accomplice.

Mulcahy, who strenuously denied the allegations, emerged as the chief perpetrator of the crimes and the first to decide that sexual stimulation was no longer enough of a thrill, leading the pair to turn to murder. He was said, by a former employee at a cab firm he worked at, to despise women.

Prosecutor Mark Dennis gave evidence in the trial of David Mulcahy as follows:

> **As they fed their newfound predilections they treated their victims as objects rather than persons. It was only a comparatively small step between the violence of the rapes and the murders, and Mulcahy was the first to take that step. He was the instigator and prime mover in the murders, and the one for whom the sexual abuse had become insufficient to satisfy.**

In the witness box, Duffy catalogued their heinous campaign of rape and murder, describing how the two friends would go out on "hunting parties" in the 1980s searching for women.

Duffy used his knowledge of the rail network to target his victims and drag them into concealed areas where they could be attacked. Duffy added:

> **We would have balaclavas and knives. We used to call it hunting. We did it as a bit of a joke. A bit of a game.**

Mulcahy protested his innocence, but on the 5 February, 2001, he was sentenced to three life sentences for murdering three women.

He also received twenty four 24-year jail terms on each of seven counts of rape and 18 years each for five conspiracies to rape, to run concurrently.

The police believed that the two men were probably responsible for more deaths and sexual attacks and reinvestigated the 1980 murder of nineteen year old Jenny Ronaldson, who was sexually assaulted, strangled and thrown in the Thames.

In the *New Society* magazine on the 4 March 1988 Canter described the techniques he used to locate where the Railway Rapist lived:

> **Many environmental psychological studies have demonstrated that people form particular mental maps of the places they use.**

Each person creates a unique representation of the place in which he lives, with its own particular distortions. In the case of John Duffy, journalists recognized his preferences for committing crimes near railway lines to the extent that they dubbed him the *Railway Rapist.*

What neither they nor the police appreciated was that this characteristic was likely to be part of his way of thinking about the layout of London, and so was a clue to his own particular mental map.

It could therefore be used to see where the psychological focus of this map was and so specify the area in which he lived.

The Duffy Mulcahy case is one of the most significant criminal cases for its first use in England of psychological offender profiling now called investigative psychology.

## THE TOWER BLOCK RAPIST CASE

The tower blocks in south Birmingham became dangerous places for elderly women between January 1986 and March 1988.

During that time seven women, some of whom were infirm, between the ages of 70-80 were viciously attacked and raped. Their attacker followed them into the elevator and overpowered them. Described by witnesses as a strong young stocky man he took them to the top floor of the tower block, sometimes carrying them up the last two flights of stairs to the landing near the roof.

Here he raped them and then escaped. Police believed that consistent patterns appeared to suggest the attacks were the work of one man.

The attacker appeared to possess a limited repertoire of locations, victims and actions. This suggested he was operating in a constrained world. Dr. David Canter was asked to assist in producing a profile of the man. Canter noticed that the tower blocks were like islands surrounded by major dual carriageways.

According to witness reports the attacker was black, athletic, without body odors and carried a sports bag. After the first offence he made no attempt to disguise himself.

This suggested that he was not afraid to be recognized in the building. He had a reason to be there. Accordingly, he had no fear that he would be recognized locally. Familiar with the location he was confident of his anonymity.

Working with crime scene investigators Canter drew up the following profile of the rapist:

> **He was non-violent and only used necessary force**
>
> **His athletic build suggested a solitary sports interest, for example, bodybuilding or swimming.**
>
> **His cleanliness and organization suggested he was obsessive.**
>
> **Because he made no attempt to avoid forensic evidence this suggested he was not aware of police procedures, meaning it was unlikely he had a previous conviction for a similar type crime. But he might have a previous conviction for some minor sexual offences.**
>
> **His ease with older women suggested he was dealing with elderly people in an non-offence context.**
>
> **His knowledge of tower blocks suggested he lived in one.**

Based on this report, a police detective searched through the records of minor sexual offenders, and found a match between Adrian Babb's fingerprints and those at the scene of crime. It was his lack of forensic awareness that led to his arrest. It turned out that Babb was a swimming pool attendant, hence the cleanliness and lack of body odor, and he looked after swimming sessions for the elderly.

It was yet another unqualified success for Canter's method of profiling.

## SO WHAT IS INVESTIGATIVE PSYCHOLOGY?

In their book *Investigative Psychology: Offender Profiling and the Analysis of Criminal Action* (2009) which is essential reading for anyone interested in learning about this approach David Canter and Donna Youngs (pictured below) describe Investigative Psychology or IP as follows:

> **Investigative psychology is the study of offenders and the processes of apprehending them and bringing them to justice.**

It deals with what all those involved in crime and its investigation, do, feel and think. The dominant objective is the understanding of crime in ways that are relevant to the conduct of criminal or civil investigations and subsequent legal proceedings.

As such, IP is concerned with psychological input to the full range of issues that relate to the management, investigation and prosecution of crime. But it is also an approach to problem solving psychology that has relevance far beyond crime and criminality.

They state that the approach is concerned with all forms of criminality and not just serial rape or killing. It extends to insurance fraud, corruption, malicious fire setting, tax evasion, smuggling and even terrorism.

Canter adopts a certain strategy that he uses within this approach to help him find the offender. He begins by trying to understand the types of crime individuals are likely to become involved in and the way the crime will be carried out. He then tries to understand the way a criminal behavior processes and how the crime mirrors their behavior in their daily life. He believes that there are associated activities that happen when a crime is being committed and that actions of offenders at the crime scene are likely to reveal something about their background.

## OPERATIONAL APPLICATIONS

Investigative psychologists are now able to inform answers to ten different classes of operation questions that confront police investigations.

## SALIENCE

What aspects of the crime are salient ones? What aspects should the police investigators focus on? If they can identify these features then it may better assist them to understand the crime and its context and lead them to the offender more speedily.

## SUSPECT ELICITATION

What searches of police records or other sources of information should investigators carry out to help them identify the offender? What are the likely dominant features of the offender? This can involve the investigation of information from databases, obtaining information from the general public and working with paid informers. All these processes can be drawn upon to generate a better understanding of the crime and the type of person who committed it.

## SUSPECT PRIORITIZATION

Which of the possible suspects are most likely to have committed the crime? A study of the crime can result in inferences about the personal characteristics and previous behavioral patterns of the offender.

This, in turn, can assist the police in distinguishing the perpetrator of a given crime from other known offenders the police may be considering. In operational terms, this becomes a question, for example, of which suspects should be drawn from police or other databases for the most detailed scrutiny. How can an investigative psychologist help here? They could give indications about the likely criminal history of an offender who has committed a certain type of crime in a certain way. This could be helpful to police searching through their lists of possible suspects.

## OFFENDER LOCATION

Where does the offender live or operate from? Where is his base? This is an important step of any investigation because ideas about where an offender is likely to be living can shape an investigation and the deployment of police personnel and resources.

Understanding the geographical patterning of an offender's criminal activities and how this relates to his or her home base has huge potential significance in operational terms. It can greatly narrow down the area in which he is most likely to be and save thousands of man hours and resources. There is more about this topic in the section on Geographical Profiling.

## CRIME LINKAGE

Which crimes are likely to have been committed by the same perpetrator? Crime linkage has many advantages for police investigations. It requires the determination of what it is about any given offender that is sufficiently internally consistent, from one crime to the next, to suggest that a single person is responsible for the crimes.

For example, if most burglars use forced entry it is unlikely that will be able to link together two burglaries committed by the same person who also happens to use forced entry. Of course, if a burglar has a *modus operandi* that is as unique to him such as a signature, then that can be used to link his crimes. But as it is uncommon for criminals to reveal their signatures it follows that issues of salience in the offender's actions are taken to a further level when crime linkage is brought into the equation.

One needs to distinguish not only the salience of the action from one offender to another but also its salience in distinguishing one offence from another.

## PREDICTION

Where and when will the offender strike again and what form might such attack take? Predicting when the offender at large will strike again is a key operation concern for crime investigators. It's not just another attack that concerns them but the likely severity of the offence, (whether there will be an escalation in violence), or whether a different form of offence is probable, is also an important matter to be considered.

## INVESTIGATIVE DECISION MAKING

How can the investigative process be improved upon? The actual details of how investigations are organized and the processes of decision making are open to psychological scrutiny. They can be influenced by knowledge of the cognitive and social processes involved which, in turn, leads on to the consideration of the most effective decision support tools and the development of such tools.

## INFORMATION RETRIEVAL

How can we make the collection of information in an investigation more effective? An understanding of the cognitive and social processes can greatly assist in such matters as the interviewing of suspects, witnesses and victims; the harnessing of information from other public and private sources; and the more efficient management of data collected. Investigative psychology can assist in all of these areas.

## EVALUATION OF INFORMATION

How can the information that becomes available be better assessed? Canter and Youngs say that the most obvious area of psychological study here is in the detection of deception. However, other aspects of the validity and reliability of information obtained is open to systematic scrutiny and improvement, particularly by drawing on psychometric tools.

## CASE PREPARATION

How can the case against the accused person be better organized from a legal standpoint? During the trial both the prosecution and defense draw implicitly on lay models and ideas about human behavior to establish their case. Formal psychological theories can be used to structure legal cases, which, in turn, can often improve the quality of arguments.

Canter and Youngs posit that psychology can contribute to these operational matter at two levels. Firstly, by providing substantive knowledge, based on empirical studies, which will lead to direct answers. Secondly, psychology can provide a framework for understanding the processes that crime investigators must go through to find the answers.

Central to the above ten operational questions are what have become known as the "profiling equations" that provide the scientific basis for inferring associations between the actions that occur during the crime and the characteristics of the offender.

The actions that occur during the crime include when and where it is committed and to whom. The offender's characteristics include his criminal history, background, base location and his relationship to others.

They use a method which they call the A to C equation. A=>C where A are the actions related to the crime; C are the characteristics of typical offenders for such crimes; and, => is the argument and evidence for inferring one from the other. Investigative psychologists use these equations to find solutions for objective bases for investigative inferences.

Canter and Youngs argue that one general hypothesis to emerge in their studies is that offenders tend to demonstrate some consistency between the nature of their crimes and characteristics they tend to exhibit in other situations.

This may be particularly helpful in linking actions and characteristics. There are several models which can be drawn on to link an offender's actions with his characteristics.

One is to examine how the offender's characteristics are the cause of the particular criminal actions. A different perspective would be to look for variables that were characteristics of the offender which would influence the particular offending actions. A third possibility is that actions give rise to some consequences from which characteristics may be inferred. For example, where particular types of goods are stolen, like jewelry, that might imply that the offender must have a relationship with other offenders who would buy or distribute those goods.

Such models avoid what Canter and Youngs, call "unnecessary assumptions" about what are often referred to as motives.

Speculations about the reasons why an offence took place can be productive but they should not be confused with empirical exploration of the correlations that underlie the relationships between actions and characteristics, and on which inferences can be based.

Canter has no time for the old fashioned detective's hunch. Assumptions should only be based on hard evidence obtained through proper tried and tested scientific processes. These inference models operate at the thematic level, rather than being concerned with particular, individual clues as would be the goal of Detective Colombo or Jessica Fletcher in *Murder She Wrote.*

This approach recognizes that a single criminal act may be unreliably recorded or may not occur because of situational factors but a group of criminal acts may indicate some dominant aspects of the offender's style which may be strongly related to some important characteristic of the offender.

In a 1997 study of 210 rapes Davies, Wittrebrod and Jackson demonstrated that if the attacker took precautions not to leave fingerprints, stole from the victims, forced entry and imbibed alcohol, then there was a very high probability that the attacker had a previous conviction for burglary.

Canter and Youngs state the classification of criminal behavioral style is central to the inference process. Police must draw on some understanding of the offender's actions in the crimes they are investigating if they are to generate leads and select from them. In order to make sense of the information they obtain they need to have some idea of typical ways in which offenders behave.

## CHANGE IN MODI OPERANDI

Canter and Youngs acknowledge and deal with a complication to the A=>C equation.

The complication relates to the fact that the way a person commits a crime usually changes over a period of time, even where there is a background of consistencies.

If you can understand how and why these changes occur then the inference process can be enhanced. In a study published in 2001 they identified five relevant forms of change.

## RESPONSIVENESS

An offender's actions may not always be the same on two different occasions simply because of the different circumstances he may face when committing a crime.

Understanding these circumstances and the offender's response to them may allow some inferences about the offender's interpersonal style or situational responsiveness to be made. These inferences may be helpful in the conduct of the investigation.

## MATURATION

Maturation is a process of change that affects us all. If we study what is typical of people at certain ages, such as sexual activity, or physical agility, then the knowledge from such study can be used to estimate the maturity of the person committing the crimes.

It can also to explain the possible basis for longer term variations in the offender's criminal activity.

## DEVELOPMENT

An offender is likely to increase his expertise in committing an offence through time. Evidence of such expertise in a crime can thus be used to help make inferences about the stages in a criminal's development that he has reached and furthermore to indicate the way their crimes might change in the future.

## LEARNING

Most offenders will learn from their earlier offending in the same way that learning theorists have shown that behavior generally is shaped by experience. So, for example, a rapist who struggled to control his first victim, may be expected to implement some very definite restraining measures during subsequent offences.

In fact, for offenders, the particularly salient, potentially negative consequences of their actions in getting caught and being sent to prison may make this a powerful process for change in the criminal context. An inferential implication of this is that it may be possible to link crimes to a common offender by understanding the logic of how behavior has changed from one offence to the next.

## CAREERS

The most general form of change that may be expected from criminals is one that may be seen as having an analogy to a legitimate career. This would imply stages such as apprenticeship, middle management, leadership and retirement.

Unfortunately the criminology literature often uses the term 'criminal career' simply to mean the sequence of crimes a person has committed.

It is also sometimes confused with the idea of a 'career criminal', someone who makes a living entirely out of crime. As a consequence much less is understood about the utility of the career analogy for criminals than might be expected.

There are some indications that the more serious crimes are committed by people who have a history of less serious crimes and consequently, the more serious a crime the older an offender is likely to be.

## MDS AND SSA

The development of a five-facet empirical classification for profiling sexual offenders was one of the earliest statistical based studies carried out by Canter and Heritage (1990).

They analyzed data from twenty seven sexual offenders involved in sixty six assaults and used this as the basis for their model. They used a method based on Facet Theory. Implementing a type of Multidimensional Scaling procedure (MDS) known as Smallest Space Analysis (SSA) (Lingoes, 1973; 1979) they identified five facets of sexual offending based on the offenders' behaviors during the commission of their offences.

The early work of Canter and Heritage (1990), and the five facets found, intimacy, sexuality, violence, impersonal and criminality, was important as a first attempt to investigate the relationship between offender behaviors and their characteristics distinct from their inferred motives. This was the main criticism of the FBI and Clinical approaches.

Since Canter's early work many other authors have emerged (e.g., Beauregard & Proulx, 2002; Canter, Hughes, & Kirby, 1998; Kocsis, Cooksey, & Irwin, 2002; Lundrigan & Canter, 2001; Porter & Alison, 2004; Porter, Woodworth, Earle, Drugge, & Boer, 2003; Santilla, Hakkanen, Canter, & Elfgren, 2003; Youngs, 2004) and produced sound research into many aspects of offender profiling.

Later, Canter (1994) found that rapists' behavior could be defined in terms of the role the victim plays for the offender, for example, person, victim or object, or vehicle in his analysis of 105 cases of rape. This finding was based on the underlying interpersonal interactions between the offender and the victim.

Canter asserts that this is distinct from any motivational factors. Building on this theme of victim role, Canter, Bennell, Alison, and Reddy (2003) suggested that rape could be classified by theme as well as by the severity and type of victim violation, for example, personal, physical, and sexual.

Four themes were classified:

1. hostility, in which the offender uses aggression and violence to demean and or humiliate his victim;

2. control, where behaviors are utilized to immobilize the victim;

3. theft, when the offender uses the opportunity for some instrumental gain; and

4. involvement, which has the offender attempting to form a pseudo-relationship with the victim. Although, almost a third of the rapes could not be classified as belonging to one theme, and a fifth mixed group was created.

In their evaluation of the Sex Offender Treatment Programme, Beech, Oliver, Fisher and Beckett (2005) classified a sample of 170 sexual offenders (112 rapists and 58 sexual murderers) into three groups according to the main motivation for their offending using MCMI-III personality profiles.

The grievance motivated offender was impulsive and vengeful and blamed others for their actions. They had low insight and were highly suspicious and resentful of others.

The sexually motivated offenders planned and fantasized about their offence beforehand, chose their victims and tended to believe that men were entitled to have sex. They tended not to be particularly impulsive, hostile or aggressive and used violence for instrumental purposes for example, to avoid detection.

The sadistically motivated offender, which consisted of sexual murderers only, was fascinated and aroused by sexual violence, such as death and or torture. They planned their offences, which often involved strangulation, mutilation and post-mortem sexual activity.

Another group Ter Beek, Van Den Eshof and Mali (2010) studied a sample of Dutch rapists with the objective of developing a statistical model that would be able to indicate the probability of predicting basic offender characteristics such as spatial behavior, living situations, and criminal history, from observable crime characteristics, consisting of *modus operandi,* victim-offender interaction, and violence.

They examined separate crime scene variables such as method of approach, verbal behavior, sexual behavior, and use of violence as well as single offender characteristics such as spatial behavior-distance travelled, living situation, and previous convictions. They discovered that their models for 'distance' and 'violence convictions' were promising. Generally speaking the study tends to support the proposition that crime characteristics can be used to indicate probable offender characteristics.

## LIMITATIONS OF THE IP APPROACH

But the investigative psychology approach is not without its critics. Copson et al. (1997) argue that statistics alone do not predict the future. They also argue that extrapolation from statistics does not support the theory that the past will be identical to the future, nor do they inherently support the underlying assumption that similar people will do things, such as committing crime, in similar ways.

They say that the use of statistics does not guarantee that the inferences drawn will be valid or reliable, because these are assuming the data, itself, is consisting of relevant and significant components, and that the statistics applied are appropriate.

Another group, Sturidsson et al. (2006) attempted to replicate Canter and Heritage's (1990) study and their development of five theoretical elements of sexual offence behaviors. They used a sample of 146 unsolved, single victim, single perpetrator sexual assault cases collected in Sweden. The motivational dimensions initially presented by Canter and Heritage using multi-dimensional scaling (MDS) were not replicated.

But this might be due to the differences between each groups' sample. Also, Sturidsson et al.'s sample were all single offence sexual offenders, whereas, some of Canter and Heritage's sample were repeat sexual offenders. This presents a problem in itself, since any apparent structure could be due to the consistency of these serial offenders.

However, a later study, Goodwill, Alison, and Humann (2009) found that Sturidsson et al.'s use of MDS was incorrect as they had used ALSCAL procedure in SPSS, which produces a dissimilarity matrix, as opposed to using the PROXSCAL procedure, which can be used to produce a similarity matrix.

This resulted in the variables of high frequency being positioned around the periphery of the plot, while low frequency variables were clustered more centrally. This meant that objects which are positioned closer together are more dissimilar, something which is inconsistent with other MDS studies (e.g., Alison & Stein, 2001; Canter & Heritage, 1999; Canter, Alison, Alison, & Wentink, 2004; Canter, Bennell, Alison, & Reddy, 2003; Mokros & Alison, 2002), where the opposite solution is utilized.

There is a question mark over the use of MDS, itself, as a statistical research method, because replication across several studies (Canter & Heritage, 1990; House, 1997; Kocsis, Cooksey, & Irwin, 2002) using similar variables has not been successful.

Highly correlated variables tend to distort MDS, with these clustering heavily in the central area of the plots and less correlated variables being pushed outwards, making it more difficult to find a meaningful interpretation.

Another problem is that by including too few variables it makes determining rapist behavior less apparent (Sturidsson et al., 2006). But it should be pointed out that these are minor issues to esoteric parts of the investigative psychology approach.

Criminal profiling in Britain is currently provided to police forces by the Association of Chief Police Officers (ACPO), and through the NCPE Crime Operations who recruit individuals as full time Behavioral

Investigative Advisors (BIAs) (Rainbow, 2007).

BIAs provide investigative support utilizing their vast experience of serious crime and the knowledge to integrate their behavioral advice into an investigation.

While, BIA still involves what is typically considered to be criminal profiling it also involves providing investigative suggestions, interview advice, risk assessment, media advice, and familial DNA prioritization. But while the involvement of BIAs in cases of serious crimes has shown to be beneficial, their involvement is best suited to crimes where sufficient offender behavior is evident and where sufficient discrimination exists between offenders within a certain crime type (Rainbow & Gregory, 2009).

# 5 GEOGRAPHICAL PROFILING

*I may not carry a detective's badge, but I'm certainly the highest ranking member of Albatross Harbor's neighborhood watch program. And like tilapia, I know something smells fishy when I taste it. In my neighborhood, nobody can take a shit in their own backyard without me knowing about it. I'm like Spencer Tracy mixed with Miss Marple, with a little maple syrup on top. I am the pancake that's served and protects, without the financial or emotional support of the community at large.*

**Jarod Kintz, *A Story That Talks about Talking Is Like Chatter to Chattering Teeth, and Every Set of Dentures Can Attest to the Fact That No..* (2011)**

## WHAT IS GEOGRAPHICAL PROFILING?

Geographic profiling is a criminal investigative technique that analyzes the locations of a connected series of crimes to help identify the probable area where a serial offender resides, or other place that serves as his anchor point or base of operations.

Implementing both qualitative and quantitative methods it helps us to understand the spatial behavior of the offender so that the search area for him can be localized to a smaller hunt area. It is primarily used in serial rape and murder cases but its effectiveness has increased its utilization to crimes such as arson, bombing and robbery.

In fact, geographic profiling also can be used in single crimes that involve multiple scenes or other significant geographic characteristics.

The process assists law enforcement agents in prioritizing information, particularly in large-scale major crime investigations involving hundreds or thousands of suspects and leads. An understanding of the spatial pattern of a crime series and the characteristics of the crime sites can help investigators determine whether the crime was opportunistic.

It also helps them understand the degree of offender familiarity with the crime location. This is based on the connection between the criminal's hunting behavior and his non-criminal life.

Police agencies around the world use several major software programs to perform geographic profiling tasks, such as Rigel®, Predator, CrimeStat, and Dragnet. These software programs can help in identifying if a series of crimes are linked, that is, carried out by the same offender or offenders.

It helps predict characteristics of the offender responsible for a series of crimes such as where they are likely to be based and what sort of knowledge they have of a particular area.

It facilitates a better understanding of the link between the crime and location as to why certain locations attract more crime than others and why, even in high crime neighborhoods, some addresses are repeatedly targeted while others are ignored.

Going forward it can assist the authorities to target crime prevention resources in the most relevant locations and in the correct and most cost effective manner.

## THE DEVELOPMENT OF GEOGRAPHICAL PROFILING

The leading developer of, and person most associated with geographical profiling is Dr. Kim Rossmo, (pictured below) who was a former detective with the Vancouver, Canada Police Department.

Picture by Nick Wilson and Matt Rainwaters

Although the process of geographical profiling in one form or another has been around for a long time (think of detectives in old movies sticking different kinds of pins into various maps) the formalized process known today as geographic profiling originated in 1989 out of research conducted at Simon Fraser University's School of Criminology in British Columbia, Canada. But before Rossmo began his research in Simon Fraser University an Englishman by the name of Professor Stuart Kind had already used a type of geographic profiling in the *Yorkshire Ripper* case almost a decade earlier.

Canter (2004) considers Kind to have been the first person to incorporate the use of geographic models into an ongoing investigation. According to Canter, Kind's work which was largely overlooked during his lifetime, went on to be considered "the origins of present-day geographical profiling." So, who was Stuart Kind?

Stuart Stanley Kind was born on the 21 January 1925 in the Meadows district of Nottingham. He was the youngest of three sons, and his father was frequently unemployed during the depression of the 1920s and 1930s. He left school at the age of fourteen. He had earlier qualified for the Mundella Grammar School in Nottingham, but his parents gave him the choice of going there or to work. He chose the latter.

He had a variety of jobs over the next four years: cinema projectionist, hatter's assistant, apprentice instrument maker, heavy lorry driver, and laboratory assistant in the pharmacy department at University College, Nottingham. At sixteen he joined the Home Guard. He later joined the RAF before studying Biology and Chemistry at Nottingham University. In 1952 he took a position as a biologist at the Home Office North Eastern Region Forensic Science Laboratory at Wakefield.

In 1954 the laboratory moved to Harrogate, where Kind carried out pioneering research on blood grouping, particularly on clothing, and developed a technique called absorption-elution.

In 1958 Kind established the forerunner of the Forensic Science Society. It held regular symposia, bringing together forensic scientists from around the world; and its journal, *Science and Justice*, became a major influence in international forensic science.

In 1969 he was appointed Director of the Forensic Science Laboratory at Newcastle. The next year he became the first forensic scientist to be elected to a Fellowship of the Institute of Biology.

In 1978 he was appointed director of the Home Office Research Establishment at Aldermaston. From 1983 he was head of the new Forensic Science Laboratory at Wetherby. But it was only during the hunt for the *Yorkshire Ripper* that Kind hit the headlines.

At 3:00 a.m. on the 9 December 1980, after less than two weeks on the case, Kind telephoned down to the reception desk at the hotel in Leeds where he and four senior detectives were billeted and asked for some graph paper and a pencil. Over the next few hours he made a series of calculations using techniques he had learned as a wartime navigator in the RAF. The *Yorkshire Ripper* had murdered thirteen women over a five-year period. Kind plotted the dates and times of the attacks on a map, with the aim of determining their "centre of gravity."

He was of the opinion that the Ripper needed darkness to cover his crimes and was trying to mislead the police as to the base of his operations. But he also knew that the Ripper had to return to his home as soon as possible afterwards to avoid capture near the scene of his crime. He therefore deduced that the earlier in the evening an attack happened, the further away from home the killer was.

From a series of calculations which were run through the computer at the Home Office Central Research Establishment at Aldermaston where Kind was the director he was able to tell his colleagues that the *Yorkshire Ripper* lived somewhere between Shipley and Bingley in West Yorkshire.

The focus of the investigation now shifted from the north-east (an area of inquiry prompted by the tape sent in by a Geordie hoaxer) to suspects in the Bradford area. One of these, the lorry driver Peter Sutcliffe, lived midway between the towns suggested by Kind. A fortnight later Sutcliffe was arrested in Sheffield by traffic police.

A decade later, across the Atlantic Ocean, Kim Rossmo began studying geographical-profiling under professors Paul and Patricia Brentingham (pictured below with their son Jeffrey) as part of his doctorate studies at Simon Fraser University. The Brentinghams had already developed a theoretical crime model which examined where crimes were most likely to happen, based on offender residence, workplace and leisure activity.

The Brentingham model maintains that we all have an "activity space" related to the areas in which we live, work and play. This activity space produces a discernible pattern of movement around the city. Therefore, it follows, that in relation to criminal activity, an offender has to know about a particular geographical area before he begins to commit his crimes.

Where the offender's movement patterns intersect within this geographical area will, to a large extent, determine where the crime takes place.

Rossmo noted that the Brentingham model was examined primarily in relation to crime prevention. But he was more interested in approaching the topic from the opposite perspective. He wanted to know what does the location of a crime say about where the offender might live?

The Brentinghams model was applied to aggregate crime patterns of hundreds of offenders. Rossmo wondered if their ideas could be reversed and applied instead to individual crimes, in particular to serial criminals. In Canada almost 75 per cent of homicides are solved, primarily because murder victims are usually attacked by someone they know like a spouse, a partner, a family member, or a work colleague. However, serial killers are a different problem. This is because usually the criminal has no previous relationship with the victim. That lack of connection makes serial crimes more difficult to solve.

The question Rossmo asked was if investigators know the location of the crimes, what can we say about where the suspect lives? Rossmo uses the analogy of a water sprinkler:

> **Take one of those rotating lawn sprinklers: it's quite difficult to predict where the next drop of water is going to fall. On the other hand, if you wait for a lot of drops of water to fall, it's much easier to work out where the sprinkler is from the pattern of the drops.**

At university, Rossmo began studying not just serial killers but quantitative geography and animal foraging patterns, among other topics. He wanted to know where the suspect goes when he's not offending, where's his comfort zone, where does he spend most of his time. Most serial crimes occur close to where a suspect lives or works or an area he used to live or work in. Basically, we're talking about an area the suspect knows well. Usually, victims are not chosen because of who they are but because they happen to be in the wrong place at the wrong time.

Rossmo believes that most crimes take place close to the suspect's home, often within a kilometer. As you move further away from their home, the probability they will offend drops off. Rossmo calls this pattern "distance decay". However, basically to protect their anonymity, criminals are also less likely to offend very near to where they live. This area is called the "buffer zone". The balance between these two tendencies can dictate where a crime is most likely to occur. However, there are variations to this pattern: adult offenders tend to travel further than do juvenile offenders; robbers tend to travel longer distances than do burglars; body dumpsites tend to be further from the killer's residence than from the sites they meet their victims.

## ROSSMO'S GEOGRAPHICAL PROFILING MODEL

It all really began to happen for Kim Rossmo in 1996. Rossmo was a detective inspector from the Vancouver Police Department (VPD). In August of that year he was contacted by a British police task force called Operation Lynx. The task force involved police officers from three counties Leicestershire, West Yorkshire and Nottinghamshire. They were all searching for a suspect whom they believed was responsible for five abductions, rapes and violent sex attacks over the previous fifteen years.

The most recent attack occurred around lunchtime in July 1995, in a multistory car park in the northern city of Leeds. A 22-year-old student was grabbed from behind while getting into her car. The suspect covered her eyes with superglue, tied her up and sexually assaulted her. However, in the process of this assault he accidentally cut himself, leaving a trace of blood in the car. Six months later, forensic scientists matched the DNA in the blood with DNA found at a crime scene in Nottingham in May 1993.

On that occasion a 23-year-old woman was abducted at knifepoint and raped. Shortly afterwards, the police linked the attacker to three more rapes that had occurred between 1982 and 1984 in Bradford, Leeds and Leicester.

It led to one of the biggest manhunts in British history: the area of the crimes and related incidents was 7,046km2 and the police had over twelve thousand suspects. The British police requested Rossmo's assistance.

Rossmo was considered something of an expert in the new area of geographic profiling, a method of tracking serial criminals which used data about the location of the crimes. Rossmo had founded VPD's first geographic profiling unit in 1995, and had a growing reputation for helping to solve difficult serial crimes using his Rigel® system of profiling.

The British police were using the case as a test to see if Rossmo's methods could transfer to Britain. Rossmo was somewhat skeptical about the use of Rigel® in the Lynx case because they only had data relating to just five rapes, which he didn't consider sufficient for an accurate analysis. Also, apart from the DNA taken from the sample of blood, the British police also had a partial fingerprint which was too small to be matched using automatic fingerprint recognition. This is a system that matches samples against a database of convicted criminals.

In May 1997 Rossmo visited the crime sites. At this stage, investigators had detained a stolen blue Ford Cortina, which the attacker used during the second rape. Inside the glove box, the rapist had found a credit card. He used the card in various shops around Leeds to purchase, *inter alia*, a video game called Scramble, a shirt, cigarettes, alcohol and a Parker pen.

Only Rossmo saw the significance in these purchases. He considered that they were all routine purchases that you would normally make near where you lived. That made him focus even more on Leeds. By using the locations of the Leeds' crimes and the Leeds' purchases, he began calculating a geographic profile using the Rigel® system. The system highlighted two areas, including the Millgarth and Killingbeck districts. Both of those districts contained their own police stations, so the investigation initiated a manual search for a fingerprint match at the two locations.

The search went on for months and the investigation began to run out of steam. They could find no match at Millgarth. But, after nearly one thousand manhours of sifting through more than 7,000 fingerprint records, they got a result. An analyst found a card at Killingbeck that matched the partial fingerprint from the Nottingham rape. They now had a suspect. His name was Clive Barwell.

Barwell was now working as a long-distance lorry driver, using his spare time to referee football matches in the Northern Counties League. He was married with three children. His fingerprints were on police records because he had been in prison from 1989 until 1995.

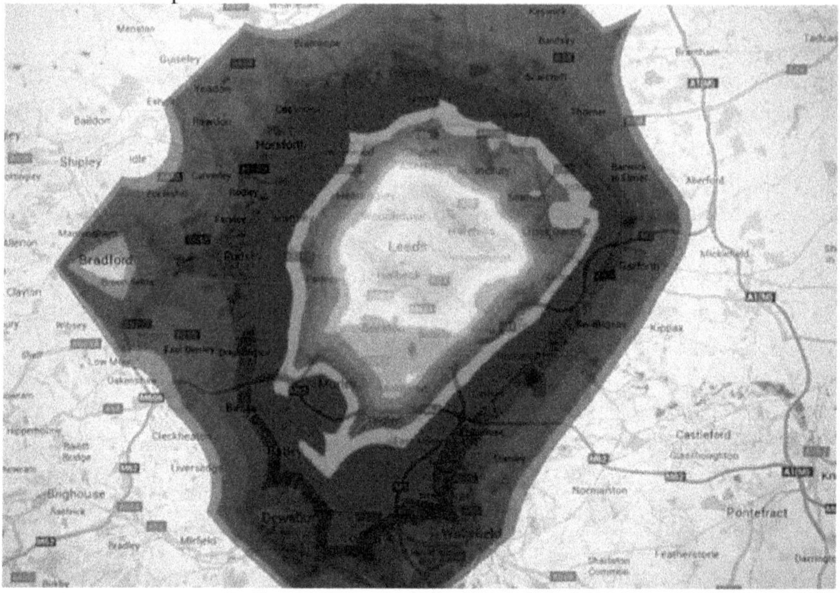

On the 6 November 1987, Barwell was arrested for using a sawn-off shotgun to rob half a dozen security vans and stealing numerous cars, including sixteen from one car park in York in a single day. On the 13 January 1989, he was sent to prison for sixteen years. The police had not begun to suspect that he was a serial rapist but they had at least locked him up where he could do no more harm to women. And yet within three and a half years, he was able to rape again, this time from within prison.

Barwell behaved like a model prisoner, obeying the rules and taking educational courses; persuading prison officers, governor grades and probation officers that he was trustworthy and reformed. In 1992 he was reduced to Category D, the lowest possible security status, and sent to an open prison in Sudbury, Derbyshire. He was immediately allowed to return home on resettlement license, which also allowed him to work locally as an electrician and to attack women.

On the 7 January 1990, he went to Leeds to visit his sick father on a four-day leave and at 22:00 he attacked a woman who was leaving her car in the city centre. The woman fought him off. She told police he had grappled her towards her car door, holding a butcher's knife at her throat and ordering her to get in, and she had no doubt he was trying to abduct her. West Yorkshire police not only failed to find her attacker but recorded the incident as an attempted robbery.

Four months later, Barwell left the prison on day release to go to work as an electrician. He travelled to Nottingham and abducted, raped and attempted to burn to death the 23-year-old woman he found in the multi-storey car park there. Although only five years into his 16-year sentence, Barwell continued to enjoy a life of liberty.

He met a 33-year-old divorcee, Margaret Teasdale. Barwell had divorced his former wife and, on Valentine's Day 1994, he and Margaret were married in Leeds' register office. The two of them then set up home not far from Sudbury prison, in the Beresford Arms hotel, in Ashbourne, where they worked as managers. Barwell slept in the hotel for up to three nights at a time and was drawing a salary of £10,400 a year. The prison service approved all these activities as part of his resettlement Programme.

West Yorkshire police made more errors. A passerby who found the victim in her car made notes of what she said, but the police lost them. An ambulance officer also made notes of what she said but destroyed them several months later when police failed to ask for a statement.

A detective inspector from Notts contacted them to suggest that the abduction of this student could be linked to the abduction of the 23-year-old woman from the multi-storey car park in Nottingham. West Yorks detectives, in the words of one police source, "told him to fuck off". However, despite all these errors, they eventually made a breakthrough with the fingerprint match. Barwell was arrested the very next day.

Barwell turned out to be a very ordinary man. If there were clues to his disposition, they lay in childhood incidents. His father frequently beat his mother in front of the children and recruited the twelve year-old Clive to keep guard on her. Eventually, his mother walked out with the other children but left Clive behind with his father who poisoned his mind against his mother in particular and women in general. Barwell had been married three times, and although he had shown some signs of violence, none of his wives had suspected his true nature.

Barwell lived in Killingbeck. His mother lived in Millgarth, the other area highlighted by the geographic profile, and he used to visit her regularly. A DNA test provided a match and, in October 1999, Barwell pleaded guilty in court. He was sentenced to eight life terms.

In an interview in *Wired* magazine in November 2014 Rossmo said this about the case:

> **The offender's residence was in the top three per cent of the geoprofile. Without any prioritization, all else being equal, the offender would have been found, on average, in the top 50 per cent of the area. During our last meeting, the detectives told me that the investigation was winding down. If the prioritization was wrong, it was unlikely Barwell would have been identified in time.**

In 1998, soon after completing his PhD, the Lafayette Police Department in Louisiana requested Rossmo to help them identify a criminal known as the *South Side Rapist.* Since 1984, a man wearing a scarf across his face had assaulted fourteen women in their homes. Apart from DNA samples from six of the sites and thousands of suspects the police had little else to go on.

Rossmo was happy to oblige. When preparing a geographic profile, Rossmo would spend hours at crime sites. Often he would go back and forth between the various crime scenes in different directions and at different times of the day. Sometimes he would walk the route sometimes drive, all in an effort to understand how one location connected to another. He would requisition weather data from the dates of the crimes and check for nearby bus stops, subway stations and bars. Rossmo says:

> **Computers can do a lot but the analyst creates the profile. When a geographic profiler works a case, it may take a week to do the profile but only half a day on the computer. The rest is reading reports and understanding what's going on. What's the hunting style of the criminal? How did the offender know about the location? What was his geographical *modus operandi*? In every case, you need to know the situation from the offender's perspective.**

In Lafayette, Rossmo accompanied by McCullan Gallien, the lead investigator, walked the streets for three days, studying the sites. There were a lot of different types of homes. There were homes in the projects, in rich neighborhoods, apartments, and single-family dwellings. Rossmo figured the suspect had a large mental map, which meant he was comfortable in a wide range of environments. Accordingly, Rossmo thought he might be a taxi driver or delivery guy. Someone who was driving through neighborhoods at night, peeping in windows and choosing his targets with care.

Using the information, Rossmo generated a geographic profile which narrowed the number of suspects to about a dozen. All twelve were cleared after taking a DNA swab test. Then the police got an anonymous tip about a sheriff's deputy called Randy Comeaux. Gallien knew him personally.

Comeaux's address was in the top eight per cent of the geoprofile. According to Rossmo this was not a great hit. However, Gallien figured that the geoprofile wasn't based on where the offender was living today. It was based on where he was living at the time of the rapes. Gallien checked the personnel records. Result! The suspect's old address was in the top one per cent of the geoprofile, an area less than 1.3km. Gallien used a discarded cigarette butt to extract Comeaux's DNA. The butt matched with the DNA found at the crime scenes. When interrogated, Randy by name and Randy by nature, Comeaux confessed.

Also in 1998, Rossmo was selected to work on a case in 1998 involving twenty seven missing women from Vancouver's downtown Eastside district, a rundown former industrial area. All the missing women were either drug addicts or sex workers or both. It was only in September 1998, after a group of community workers began demanding an investigation into the matter, that the Vancouver Police Department initiated an official search for the missing women.

Prior to 1995 there were only a few reports of missing persons who had not been found. However, after that the numbers rose significantly. Rossmo considered that this was similar to what epidemiologists would call a spatial-temporal cluster; in other words, there were too many events, in too small an area, in too short a period of time, for this just to be random. If these were disease reports, the cluster would indicate an epidemic.

Detective constable Lori Shenher from the missing-persons unit was assigned to the case. Shenher spoke to friends and relatives of the missing women, eventually locating two of them, but also adding thirty seven more to the list of missing persons. At this point, family and friends of the women asked the police board to offer a reward of $100,000 for information regarding a possible serial killer prowling the Eastside area. The reward was equal to what had already been offered for a series of residential robberies on the city's affluent west side. The mayor of Vancouver rejected the proposal, stating that he wasn't financing a "location service for hookers". However, after sustained media pressure, a reward was eventually offered. But the mayor's attitude was indicative of what a lot of people thought, citizens and police officers. These were just hookers, throwaway people.

In May 1999, Rossmo presented a report to Fred Biddlecombe, the inspector in charge of the VPD's major-crime section. But Bidddlecombe had his own theories. He thought the sex workers would be found, that they had overdosed, that their pimps had killed them. Each one of his theories was more ridiculous than the next. It never seemed to dawn on him to ask the obvious questions. Why only women? Why only in that area? Why no bodies? Rossmo's analysis suggested that they were dealing with a serial killer. Tensions grew. In December 2000, the Vancouver Police Department refused to renew Rossmo's contract as a geographic profiler and offered him a reduced rank. Rossmo left.

Serial killer Robert Pickton continued to hunt, butcher, destroy and dispose of Vancouver's sex workers with impunity. Who was Pickton?

Robert William Pickton (pictured below) was Canada's most prolific rapist and serial killer who slaughtered forty nine women, mostly drug addicted, sex workers and fed them to the pigs on his farm. He was convicted of six murders and boasted of forty nine. His first criminal trial took over a year. His trial and conviction has so far cost the Canadian state almost $80,000,000.

A battery of expensive defense lawyers, paid for by the former multi-millionaire pig farmer, secured a conviction of second degree murder for him in only six of the forty nine suspected murders he allegedly committed. They persuaded the Judge to withhold evidence from the jury which they claimed would have been prejudicial to a fair trial.

In a hugely controversial judgment the trial judge, Judge Williams, held that the first case should proceed with only six charges of murder and the balance remain for a second trial.

Willie Pickton was born on the 24 October 1949 in Port Coquitlam in British Columbia in Canada. Port Coquitlam is forty minutes southeast of Vancouver. His parents were Leonard and Helen Louise Pickton and he had one brother called Dave and a sister called Linda. His parents were pig farmers from a long line of pig farmers. In 1905, Willie's great-grandfather, also called William, purchased a parcel of land adjacent to a mental hospital and raised hogs. When his children grew up they raised hogs, and when their children's children grew up they raised hogs, all on the very same farm. Then in the late 1950s, due to the intended construction of the Lougheed Highway the Picktons were forced to sell their farm and move.

In 1963 they bought forty acres of swamp land for $18,000 at 953 Dominion Avenue later to become Vancouver's Ground Zero. They towed their modest blue and white mobile home to the site and set about raising hogs and a family. While Linda was sent to a boarding school in the city the two boys went to local schools and spent every single hour of their spare time working on the farm. Willie lived with the pigs, worked with the pigs, built up the pigs, slept with the pigs and eventually slaughtered the pigs.

The father, Leonard, died in 1978 and their mother died the following year, leaving the farm to the two boys and Linda. But it was the boys who took over the farm with David as manager and Willie as farm hand. It was hard work and they claim they were, at this time, dirt poor. In 1993, the Pickton's swamp land was valued at $300,000 but the following year due to its suitability for housing, it was re-valued at $7,200,000. Part of the farm was sold to a construction company called Eternal Holdings for $1,700,000 to develop townhouses. Also in 1992 Port Coquitlam bought a parcel of the land for $1,200,000 and turned it into a park. In 1995 Port Coquitlam's school district bought a further parcel for $2,300,000 and built Blakeburn Elementary School. In three years the fortunes of Willie and Dave Pickton were transformed from dirt poor pig farmers to multimillionaires.

Around about the same time women began to go missing at an alarming rate from the DES (Vancouver's Downtown Eastside). In 1995, Catherine Gonzales disappeared followed by Catherine Knight, Dorothy Spence, Diana Melnick, Tanya Holyk, Olivia Williams, Frances Young, Stephanie Lane, Helen Hallmark, and Janet Henry; and that was just the beginning.

After selling off most of the land Willie's brother Dave moved out of the family home to 2552 Burns Road about a mile away where he opened a recreational center called Piggy's Palace. Like the Pickton brothers themselves, Piggy's Palace, led a double life. Registered as a "non-profit" organization its founding aims were to raise money for "sports organizations and other worthy groups."

The Palace was simply a sparsely furnished, dimly-lit, long tin shed but initially it was visited by ordinary decent people from Port Coquitlam who enjoyed the roasted pork on the spit barbeques, parties and functions. But soon it was the place for booze, bikers, hookers, ex-cons, drugs and orgies. The Picktons supplied the Palace with all the pig roast from their hog farm. The Palace only sold whole hogs roasted on the spit. You could see what you were eating and be sure where it came from. But you couldn't be sure what those pigs had been eating.

Those parts of the pigs which they couldn't openly sell to the public, that is, intestines, brains, nerves, entrails and bones, were transported by truck to West Coast Reduction, a modern impressive rendering plant close to DES at 105 North Commercial Drive. Most commentators believe that the partial remains of Pickton's victims were included in these deliveries. This huge plant transforms animal bones, guts, fish, blood, pig entrails and used restaurant grease into consumer products like soaps, shampoos and lipstick. It also transforms them into animal feed.

The plant would have had no way of knowing that Pickton's deliveries contained human body parts. Pickton was known to make his deliveries and then pick up prostitutes within a block of the plant and bring them back to his farm where, according to witnesses, he tortured, raped and later butchered them. He then mutilated their bodies and fed them to his pigs.

Pickton picked up most of the sex workers in the DES area of Vancouver. He used to hang out in the seedy hotels like the Roosevelt Hotel and the Astoria Hotel. He visited alone, drank alone and always left with a woman who was invariably a drug addict on the game. A wannabe biker or badass Pickton was regarded by those who knew him as a slimy weasel who suffered from serious personal hygiene problems. Most people were unaware of his criminal background.

In 1997 Pickton picked up a prostitute and drug addict called Wendy Lynn Eistetter in Dominion Avenue. He tried to handcuff her and then repeatedly stabbed her with a brown handle knife. She managed to escape from him at 1:45 a.m. by fleeing partially naked and covered in blood onto the street where she was assisted by a passer-by and brought to hospital. Pickton was charged on the 23 March 1997 with attempted murder but the charges were later dropped because prosecutors thought they would have difficulty in securing a conviction. After he was freed, over thirty more prostitutes went missing from the DES area. Pickton was responsible for the slaughter of many of them.

It took a long time to eventually catch Willie Pickton due in part to the indifference of the Canadian police to the plight of the victims. They were not "respectable" professionals or housewives. They were women who were forced to feed their addiction by prostitution. Only their families cared about these poor unfortunate women. Another reason why he wasn't caught sooner was the incompetence of both the RCMP (Royal Canadian Mounted Police) and the Vancouver Police Department who failed to pool information each department had on the case or consider the geographical profiling reports, all of which resulted in the slaughter of more innocent lives.

On the 5 February 2002 in their investigation into the alarming number of missing women from Vancouver the RCMP served a search warrant on Pickton. They didn't find any of the missing women but they did eventually find body parts, lots of them, like hands, feet and heads, in freezers. Also found were dozens of women's clothes, personal effects, and teeth. The *New York Times* edition of the 23 November 2003 wrote:

> **A special team investigating the cases arrived and found body parts in a freezer, as well as purses and other personal effects later linked to the missing.... Not one body has been found intact, and a wood chipper and Mr. Pickton's pigs are believed to have devoured much of the evidence.**

For years it was not possible to write about the evidence found on the farm due to Canada's peculiar restriction on news reporting involving ongoing trials. But the animal rights organization PETA circumvented the ban and placed a full page advertisement in the Province outlining what Pickton had done to his victims:

> **They were drugged and dragged across the room. Their struggles and cries went unanswered. They were slaughtered and their heads were sawed off. Their body parts were refrigerated. And their bones discarded. It's Still Going On. Remember that this scenario is a reality for more than 640 million sensitive individuals who lose their lives every year in this country for nothing more than the taste of their 'meat.'**

But we now know that the reality was even worse than this. The six murders of which Pickton was convicted on the 9 December 2007 relate to the slaughter of the following women: twenty nine year old Sereena Abotsway who disappeared in August 2001; twenty six year old Mona Lee Wilson who went missing on the 30 November 2001; twenty two year old

Andrea Joesbury who was last seen on the 8 June 2001; thirty two year old Brenda Ann Wolfe, who was last seen in February 1999; Marnie Lee Frey, last seen in August 1997; and Georgina Faith Papin, last seen in January 1999.

Pickton's robust defense team succeeded in persuading an over-sensitive Judge Williams to withhold the following evidence from the jury at the trial of these six ladies. The evidence relates to the other twenty murder charges he faced concerning the slaughter of twenty other victims. Reporting on this evidence was restricted until the Canadian Supreme Court quashed the killer's bid for a new trial.

DNA belonging to ten of the victims was discovered in items found in two freezers in Pickton's workshop, the same place where investigators found the mutilated body parts of two women he was convicted of killing. There were also packages of ground meat in the freezer which contained the DNA of victims Inga Hall and Cindy Feliks. Furthermore, the DNA of Cara Ellis was found on Pickton's jacket and Andrea Borhaven's DNA on his boots.

Police found dozens of personal effects on Pickton's farm and trailer belonging to the twenty additional victims including Jennifer Furminger's DNA on a saw in the slaughterhouse; the DNA of both Pickton and victim Jacqueline McDonell on handcuffs in the killer's bedroom, and Pickton's DNA on two condoms found inside two purses linked to Sarah de Vries and Dianne Rock. The partial leg bone of victim Wendy Crawford was uncovered in the cistern of the old piggery, near the remains of two women Pickton was convicted of killing.

The prosecution had also argued that Pickton's blow-up sex doll found in his bedroom closet near items belonging to the victims was relevant because "of the potential sexual nature of Mr. Pickton's dealings" with the women. However, Judge Williams held that the admission of the sex toy would be prejudicial to the accused's character adding:

> **The doll in question is rather peculiar and bizarre in appearance. The thought that Mr. Pickton engaged in sexual activity with this item could reasonably be expected to repulse members of the jury. In my view, there is a real concern that admission of the doll would be prejudicial, as it could lead the jury to conclude that Mr. Pickton is a sexually maladjusted individual and a person of bad character.**

Williams also excluded portions of a videotape of the killer immediately after his arrest on the 22 February 2002, in his cell with a cellmate who was actually an undercover policeman. When the cellmate was briefly removed, Pickton stripped off his clothes and masturbated in his jail cell, despite knowing that he was being recorded on a security camera in the ceiling.

One of the most frequent questions among commentators on the Pickton serial killings is whether or not Willie Pickton acted alone or with others in the killing of at least sixty victims. Vancouver Police Department had excluded the possibility that American serial killer Gary Ridgway was responsible. Although Ridgway operated south of Vancouver in nearby Seattle and often visited Vancouver police discounted him earlier on. It's possible that a proper geographical profile of both Ridgway and Pickton might have linked them together. However, they found it more difficult to discount Pickton's brother, Dave, whose bedroom contained multiple sex toys, including one bearing the DNA of an unidentified woman whose DNA was also found in one of the slaughterhouse freezers.

Three of Willie Pickton's friends were suspects at one time or another; Lynn Ellingsen, Pat Casanova and Dinah Taylor. All three were arrested but never charged in the case. Police said there was no evidence to support the laying of criminal charges. RCMP Staff Sgt. Wayne Clary testified that Ellingsen was arrested because information she gave to police in August 1999 about seeing a butchered body in Pickton's slaughterhouse had not yet been confirmed.

Thirty seven year old Ellingsen, a former friend of the killer, was a key prosecution witness who testified that she saw a dead woman strung up like a pig's carcass and hanging from a chain in Pickton's barn. She said that she had been living on the farm and doing odd jobs for Pickton for a couple of months when one night the pair went out cruising the Vancouver streets looking for a prostitute for Pickton.

She said they brought one woman back to the Port Coquitlam farm. Ellingsen told the court while the woman and Pickton went in one room, she went into another and got high on drugs. She woke up when she heard a noise and saw a bright light coming from the barn next door where Pickton slaughtered pigs. She went to look:

> **I saw this body. It was hanging. Willie pulled me inside, behind the door. Walked me over to the table. Made me look. Told me if I was to say anything, I'd be right beside her.**

She told the court that the woman hanging in the barn was the person they had picked up earlier that night:

> **This woman that we had picked up, at my eye level was where her feet, like her legs were, I seen red toe nail polish. On this big shiny table, I don't know what it was, but it was lots of blood and uh, hair, black hair.**

When the prosecution counsel asked if she had seen the victim's face she answered: "Not her face, but it was her hair, like she had long black hair and that's what was laying on the table. I just remember her toes." When asked if the killer was doing anything to the woman, she said: "There were knives with blood on them. He was full of blood himself.

Clary said the same could be said of Casanova, but added no evidence linking any of the three to the killings was ever found. Casanova was subjected to surveillance, wiretap, polygraph, and a police undercover operation but there was insufficient evidence to convict him. The prosecution believed that Pickton acted alone when he killed six women on his Port Coquitlam property. The defense, however, tried to implicate Taylor as the perpetrator particularly in relation to the murder of Andrea Joesbury.

Robert William Pickton was eventually convicted of six second degree murders and sentenced by Supreme Court Judge James William on the 11 December 2007 to twenty five years in prison without the possibility of parole. In sentencing him the Judge added: "Mr. Pickton's conduct was murderous and repeatedly so. I cannot know the details but I know this: What happened to them was senseless and despicable."

In 2010, a commission of inquiry was set up to investigate the role of the Vancouver Police Department and the Royal Canadian Mounted Police in the Pickton case. Rossmo was called to testify:

> **What happened was the equivalent of a fire station refusing to send out firetrucks because they only see smoke but no fire. All I did was a simple quantitative analysis but Biddlecombe's mind was already made up. I wasn't going to be able to convince him.**

When the final report of the Missing Women Commission of Inquiry was submitted in June 2012, it read:

> **It is difficult to understand the continued currency of nonsensical theories, such as extended vacations or a sudden rise in deaths due to overdoses without leaving a trace. Senior police officers appeared to consider Detective Inspector Rossmo's analysis to be 'speculative' despite the fact that it was grounded in solid empirical evidence and**

**factual analysis.**

Few agents are fully qualified to deal with serial-killer cases. The training takes nearly two years. There are only a handful in Britain. Colin Johnson (pictured below) was one such agent.

Picture by Nick Wilson and Matt Rainwaters

He studied under Neil Trainor, who in 1999 was the first British detective to study under Rossmo. Johnson has worked, for instance, in the case of the *M25 rapist* Antoni Imiela.

By September 2002, police had identified the existence of an extremely dangerous serial rapist who, an hour after one attack, had used the victim's mobile phone to call her mother and taunt her. mother. Dubbed the "Summer Rapist" and the "Trophy Rapist" because he sometimes stole items of clothing having forced his victims to strip, Imiela's *modus operandi* was to approach his victims at speed from behind. He always carried a knife and if a victim resisted they were punched in the face.

Kent Police and Surrey Police launched a joint investigation codenamed Operation Orb and Imiela was finally caught with the use of geographical profiling. Once police had his DNA they launched a public appeal for information which resulted in a woman coming forward who expressed suspicion about her neighbor. A DNA swab test was carried out on the individual, Antoni Imiela, which enabled police to link him to the attacks. He was subsequently arrested.

On the 4 March 2004, he was sentenced to seven life sentences (with eight years minimum) at Maidstone Crown Court for the crimes. Then on the 18 October 2010, Imiela was charged with the rape, indecent assault and buggery of a 29 year old woman, Sheila Jankowitz, on Christmas day 1987 in Forest Hill, south east London. Imiela (pictured below) was found guilty of the rape, indecent assault and sexual assault of Jankowitz on 22 March 2012 and was sentenced to a further twelve years in prison

All in all, Imiela had, in the space of a year, attacked at least ten women and girls. The area of the attacks spread over 9,000km2. Using Rigel®, Johnson generated a geographic profile that identified a 31-kilometre-square area around Woking, Surrey. Commenting on the case, Johnson told *Wired*:

> **Usually the profile identifies an area around the home of the offender, but this was different. I believed it was his workplace. Most offences occurred on weekdays in working hours. And we had two offences on one day which indicated he was commuting to the south. The analysis also suggested that the rapist lived in or close to Ashford, where he had committed his first offence, and which, unlike the other attacks, had occurred after dark. It was likely to be an opportunistic attack which he hadn't planned. After that, he was aware that the police had his DNA profile so he avoided that area.**

Nearly a year into the investigation, the police made a television appeal on TV's *Crimewatch*. They received more than 10,000 calls, including one from Imiela's neighbor, Kathy Sherwood. Johnson added:

> **His profile fitted the geography. We had two key points at a considerable distance apart, one in Woking and another in Ashford. Not too many people have a connection with both.**

In fact, Imiela lived with his wife Christine in the village of Appledore, 16km southwest of Ashford, and he worked for a Woking-based company. On November 21, 2002, the police took Imiela's DNA. It took two weeks for the police to match it with their forensic samples, after which he was swiftly arrested. Two days after the DNA swab, Imiela committed a final crime. He travelled to Birmingham and attacked a ten-year-old, telling her: "I've got nothing to lose."

Rossmo's latest book, *Criminal Investigative Failures*, analyses the various cognitive biases that affect investigations, such as the Vancouver case.

Shortly after Operation Lynx, Britain's National Crime and Operations Faculty sent one of its detectives to study under Rossmo and learn his techniques. In 2000, the organization opened the first British geographic profiling unit. Today, geographic profiling is used in tens of top-tier crimes every year in Britain, not only in high-profile cases but also ones as diverse as a series of arson attacks on wheelie bins and houses in Chester-le-Street, near Durham, and in the case of a man responsible for 23 knife-point robberies in south London.

Since Operation Lynx, Rossmo's innovative methods have increasingly become part of criminal investigations around the world. More than 725 people from 350 police agencies, including the Royal Canadian Mounted Police, the FBI, the Bureau of Alcohol, Tobacco, Firearms and Explosives and the UK's National Crime Agency, have been trained as geographic profilers. Recently, Environmental Criminology Research Inc (ECRI), the company cofounded by Rossmo, has sold Rigel® to Shandong State police, the first crime agency in China to buy the software.

Colin Sutton, a former senior investigating officer of the Metropolitan Police Murder Squad who led several high profile investigations is a huge fan of geographical profiling. Also speaking to *Wired* he said:

> **Geographic profiling a serial criminal makes a lot more sense than the more traditional psychological profiling. I fail to easily recall an instance where psychological profiling has assisted an officer in solving a series of serious crimes. Whereas geographical profiling is a much more exact science that can help target resources and target our enquiries into a specific place.**

How does it work? Rather than trying to calculate the exact location of the offender's home, which was unrealistic, Rossmo decided to devise a mathematical algorithm that, given a map with various locations associated with a series of crimes, could calculate the most probable location for the offender's residence. He had a breakthrough in 1991, during a research project in Japan about community policing. A formula jumped out of his head and he wrote it on a napkin.

The algorithm, called criminal geographic targeting, was later developed into Rigel®. To use Rigel®, a geographic profiler first enters the crime locations using a computerized map. The software then lays a 40,000-pixel grid over the area of the crimes. For each pixel, the software adds a probability function that mathematically expresses the interplay between the buffer zone and the distance decay. The function, according to Rossmo, looks like "a volcano with a caldera" Rigel® then adds the probabilities for all the crime locations, outputting a probability surface across the map. The map is visually similar to a topographic map, but instead of elevations, each point depicts the likelihood the offender is based there. The peak of that topography represents the point where the serial killer is likely to begin his hunt from, in most cases his home.

Rossmo says criminal geographic targeting, CGT, helps assess the spatial characteristics of crimes.

Basically, the system analyzes the geographic coordinates of the offender's crimes and produces a color map which assigns probabilities to different points for the most likely area of the criminal's operating base.

CGT has been patented and integrated into a specialized crime analysis software product. The Rigel® product is developed by a software company co-founded by Rossmo called Environmental Criminology Research Inc.

CGT uses overlapping distance-decay functions centered on each crime location to produce jeopardy surfaces. These are three-dimensional probability surfaces that indicate the area in which the offender is probably based. The distance-decay concept supposes that people, including criminals, generally take more short trips and fewer long trips in the course of their daily lives, which may include criminal activities.

These areas can become a comfort zone for predatory offenders to commit their crime with a feeling of safety. Consequently, criminal acts can follow a distance-decay function, such that the further away the regular activity space of an offender is, the less likely that the person will engage in a predatory criminal activity.

However, there is also a buffer zone where an offender will usually avoid committing crimes too close to their homes in the likely event that they will be identified by a neighbor.

Overlapping distance-decay functions are sets of curves expressing this phenomenon and suggesting, for example, that it is more likely that offenders live close to the sites of their crimes than far away. Probability surfaces are usually displayed on both two- and three-dimensional color isopleth maps.

Rigel® will produce a topographic map based on the locations of a series of similar crimes. This map shows the "jeopardy surface," or likelihood that some area is the offender's home or operation base.

It is then superimposed on a street map on which the crimes are pinpointed, which are thought of as "fingerprints" of the offender's cognitive map.

To provide these results, CGT takes into account known movement patterns, comfort zones, and hunting patterns. For example, right-handed criminals who are trying to escape in a hurry usually escape to the left, and will discard weapons to the right. When lost, males go downhill while females go uphill.

Rossmo prefers to work with a psychological profile as part of the data. He believes that a geographical analysis highlights the crime location, any physical boundaries that were present, and the types of roads that are used for both abduction and body dump sites.

He also notes the importance of the routine activity of the victims, because people tend to stick with familiar territory. That means that an analysis of all the crime scenes could provide clues about where an offender lives.

Just like psychological profilers, geographical profilers are also trying to determine how sophisticated and organized an offender is, whether the crime was planned or opportune, and whether the offender approached a high or low risk victim. But they take it a step further in using objective measurements to pinpoint as precisely as possible the locus of criminal activity.

The construction of a geographical profile generally involves, *inter alia*:

• Complete familiarity with the case file;

• An examination of the crime scenes;

• Interviews with investigators and witnesses;

• A detailed study of area maps; and

• A computerized analysis of neighborhood demographics for both the abduction site and body dump site.

Initially Rossmo experimented with his program on cases that had already been solved in an attempt to see just how accurate it was.

For example, in 1981, Robert Clifford Olson was arrested in Vancouver for picking up two hitchhikers. Later, he confessed to eleven murders, mostly young girls and boys. Rossmo generated a map of his crimes and pinpointed within a four square block area where Olson had actually lived.

Rossmo prefers to work with at least five crimes in a clearly linked series to analyze, or at least five crime activity sites. Utilizing that information and records such as suspect lists, police reports, and motor vehicle information, he inputs information into his program and builds from there, adding new data where it emerges.

When entering the data for analyzing the geographical patterns, the principle elements involved are:

Distance

Mental Maps

Mobility

Locality demographics

Central to the concept of geographical profiling is the fact that there is a difference between perceived distance and actual distance. Certain matters can influence how this disparity can affect the commission of a crime. Everyone's perception of distance varies. How distance is perceived can be influenced by different things like the availability of transportation, the number of barriers involved (bridges, state boundaries), the type of roads (highways or by-ways), and familiarity with a specific region.

Another significant factor in geographical profiling is the concept of a mental map. A mental map is a cognitive image of one's surroundings that is developed through experiences, travel routes, reference points, and centers of activity. Those places in which we feel safe and take for granted are within our mental maps. As offenders grow in confidence they grow bolder, their maps can change and they may then increase their range of criminal activity.

Some criminals are geographically stable (stay in a certain region) and some are transient (travel around). Whether they tend toward stability or mobility depends a lot on their experience with travel, means for getting places, sense of personal security, and predatory motivations.

The mental map may also be dependent on whether the killer is a hunter, stalker, or has some other mode of attack, since the type of approach used on a victim also has a relationship to the location of the offender's operation base.

Rossmo states that an offender has four different types of style:
He may be a hunter who searches for a specific victim in a home territory;
He may be a poacher who travels away from home for hunting;
Then there is the troller who engages in opportunistic encounters while occupied in other activities; and finally,
the trapper who creates a situation to draw a victim to him.

Any one of these offender types might attack the victim upon encounter, or follow a victim before attacking, or entice the victim toward a more controlled area.

Dr. Kim Rossmo's methods have changed the way serial crime is tackled. They're disrupting how we address a vast range of problems, from epidemics to terrorism. Rossmo now heads the Centre for Geospatial Intelligence and Investigation at Texas State University. In the past he has worked with US Border Control, using Rigel® to identify illegal-immigration patterns. Military analysts have used geographic profiling to detect enemy bases from the locations of IEDs and rocket-propelled grenade attacks in Iraq and Afghanistan. In 2007, Rossmo visited Istanbul and Ankara, Turkey, where he inspected the sites associated with the assassination of a former minister of justice in the capital.

Rossmo believes that even terrorists have spatial patterns. He claims to have found strong geographic patterns in terrorists' networks and can use the ideas of geographic profiling to evaluate counter-terrorism intelligence. One of Rossmo's closest collaborators is Steve Le Comber. Steve is a mathematician at Queen Mary University in London.

Rossmo and Le Comber recently used Rigel® to find the home of Otto and Elise Hampel, a couple who secretly distributed anti-Nazi propaganda during the second world war. It was also with Le Comber that Rossmo discovered one of Rigel's most surprising applications. Out of curiosity they applied it to biology. Le Comber:

> **I didn't really think it would work but it does. You can apply it to, say, bat foraging and invasive species. Its most interesting application is in epidemics. We tested it on an outbreak of malaria in Cairo and managed to find the breeding sites of the mosquitoes.**

At the moment Le Comber is working with Public Health England and the Department of Environment, Food and Rural Affairs, using Rigel® to fight infectious diseases. The applicability of geographic profiling to the natural world is perhaps a testament that there are few patterns more universal than the way humans and animals move, search and hunt. Our relation to geography, with its reliance on routine and the principle of least effort, is fundamentally predictable.

This is the reason that the geographical component of a crime can be a crucial part of a strategy to solve it. A geographic profiler might not solve cases, only a confession, a witness or physical evidence can prove guilt, but when you have thousands of suspects and very little data, as in the case of Operation Lynx, then geographical profiling can be vital.

For environmental criminologists, crime locations are important clues, where the criminal and victim first met, where the abduction took place, where the murder happened, where the body was dumped. For a crime to have occurred the offender and the victim had to come together in time and space.

## WHAT TYPE OF QUESTIONS WILL THE GEOGRAPHICAL PROFILER ASK

Generally speaking the geographical profiling will ask the following types of questions:

Why did he pick his victims from a particular neighborhood?

Why did he pick the dump site (in the case of murder)?

What route must he have used?

When did he use this route?

How is the route generally employed by others?

What do the attractions of this route say about him?

In the case of a series of crimes, what are the geographic patterns?

Are there escape routes?

Was the area where the victim was taken appropriate for predatory activities?

Was the victim attacked in the same place that he or she was encountered?

Was the vehicle used in the attack also dumped somewhere?

There are some geographic profilers who are so confident in this approach that they believe it supersedes the methods used in psychological profiling.

## KEY CONCEPTS IN GEOGRAPHICAL PROFILING

Here are some of the key concepts in geographical profiling.

## JOURNEY TO CRIME

The Journey to Crime (Jtc) routine is an application of location theory, a framework for identifying optimal locations from a distribution of markets, supply characteristics, prices and events.

It is a distance-based method which makes estimates about the likely residential location of a serial offender. The concept supports the notion that crimes are likely to occur closer to an offender's home and follow a distance-decay function with crimes less likely to occur the further away an offender is from their home base.

It is concerned with the 'distance of crime' and that offenders will, in general, travel limited distances to commit their crimes.

Studies have shown that the journey to crime is typically very short and that criminals generally commit crimes within one or two miles of their homes.

For example, Andy Brumwell, a crime analyst with England's West Midlands Police, carried out an analysis of 258,074 crime trips made over a two year period.

He made some interesting findings, for example, about half the journeys were less than a mile. While in most U.S. studies the journeys might be a little longer because of lower population densities and greater access to vehicles. He also found that distance traveled varied with the offense. For example, shoplifters tended to travel further than many other kinds of offenders.

Females traveled further than males, possibly because many committed shoplifting and individual offenders varied considerably in crime trips. Some usually committed crimes in their local neighborhoods. Others traveled further, particularly when working with co-offenders. The youngest offenders committed crime very close to home, while those in their twenties traveled the furthest.

## RATIONAL THEORY CHOICE

RTC is based on the fundamental principle that people freely choose their behavior and are motivated by the avoidance of pain and the pursuit of pleasure. Individuals evaluate their choice of actions in accordance with each option's ability to produce advantage, pleasure and happiness.

Rational choice provides a micro perspective on why criminals decide to commit specific crimes; criminals choose to engage in crime because it can be rewarding, easy, satisfying and fun. The central premise of this theory is that people are rational beings whose behavior can be controlled or modified by a fear of punishment.

In this way, it is believed criminals can be persuaded to desist from offending by intensifying their fear of punishment. In terms of setting the quantum of punishment, according to this theory, sanctions should be limited to what is necessary to deter people from choosing crime (Siegel and McCormick, 2006).

Rational choice is based on the belief that crime is a personal choice, the result of individual decision-making processes. Individuals are responsible for their choices and thus individual offenders are subject to blame for their criminality. The theory posits that criminals weigh the potential benefits and consequences associated with committing a crime and then make a rational choice on the basis of this evaluation.

Therefore, before committing a crime, the reasoning criminal will carefully consider the chances of getting caught, the severity of the expected penalty and the value to be gained by committing the act.

Consequently, if criminals perceive the costs to be too high, the act to be too risky, or the payoff to be too small, then they will refrain from committing the crime.

The tenets of this theory are based on a number of assumptions about the decision-making process and behavioral motivations. It is held that people decide to commit crime after careful consideration of the costs and benefits of behaving in a certain manner.

This involves considering both personal factors, which may include a need for money, revenge, or entertainment, and situational factors such as the target/victim's vulnerability and the presence of witnesses, guardians, or the police.

Rational choice focuses on the opportunity to commit crime and on how criminal choices are structured by the social environment and situational variables.

## ROUTINE ACTIVITY THEORY

Routine activities theory is a subsidiary of rational choice theory. Originally developed by Cohen and Felson (1979), the primary principle of Routine Activity Theory (RAT) is that the offender and victim must intersect in time and space for a crime to occur.

Routine activity theory is one of the main theories of "environmental criminology". The theory states that a crime occurs when the following three elements come together in any given space and time: firstly, an accessible target; secondly, the absence of capable guardians that could intervene; and thirdly, the presence of a motivated offender.

An accessible target can include a person, an object or a place.

A capable guardian has a 'human element', that is usually a person who, by their mere presence, would deter potential offenders from committing a crime. But a capable guardian could also be CCTV, providing that someone is monitoring it at the other end of the camera at all times.

Examples of capable guardians include security guards, police patrols, door staff, vigilant staff and co-workers, friends and neighbors.

Routine activity theory looks at crime from an offender's point of view. A crime will only be committed if a likely offender thinks that a target is suitable and a capable guardian is absent. It is the offender's assessment of a situation that determines whether a crime will take place.

This approach focuses on the concept that crime occurs when an opportunity is taken within both parties' non-criminal spatial activity. An activity space may consist of the regular areas an offender travels such as work, school, home or recreational areas.

Routine activity theory introduces an important tool in crime analysis called the crime triangle or problem analysis triangle.

The crime triangle analyses both the elements of crime like target, location, and offender and potential responses and interventions for each of the elements of the crime.

## CRIME PATTERN THEORY

Paul and Patricia Brentingham developed this theory which suggests that crime sites and opportunities are not random. There is an emphasis in the interaction between the offender's mental map of spatial surroundings and the allotment of victims (target backcloth).

Furthermore, serial crimes are the easiest to develop geographic profiles, since each crime contains new spatial information and provides additional data including the fact that crime area tends to enlarge with an increase of comfort and confidence. The initial hunt and criminal acts are most likely to occur relatively close to the location of the offender's home or workplace. As the success rate increases, there will be a burgeoning sense of confidence to seek his prey further from home and to travel a greater distance.

Crimes that are suitable for analysis are those that are predatory in nature and exercises some spatial decision-making process such as the area for hunting targets, travel routes, mode of transportation and even body dump sites.

Their model contains eight sets of rules:

Rule 1

As individuals move through a series of activities they make decisions. When activities are repeated frequently, the decision process becomes regularized. This regularization creates an abstract guiding template. For decisions to commit a crime this is called a crime template.

Rule 2
Most people do not function as individuals, but have a network of family, friends and acquaintances. These linkages have varying attributes and influence the decisions of others in the network.

Rule 3
When individuals are making their decisions independently, individual decision processes and crime templates can be treated in a summative fashion, that is, average or typical patterns can be determined by combining the patterns of individuals.

Rule 4
Individuals or networks of individuals commit crimes when there is a triggering event and a process by which an individual can locate a target or a victim that fits within a crime template. Criminal actions change the bank of accumulated experience and alter future actions.

Rule 5
Individuals have a range of routine daily activities. Usually these occur in different nodes of activity such as home, work, school, shopping, entertainment or time with friends that are nodes of activity and along the normal pathways between these nodes.

Rule 6
People who commit crimes have normal spatio-temporal movement patterns like everyone else. The likely location for a crime is near this normal activity and awareness space.

Rule 7
Potential targets and victims have passive or active locations or activity spaces that intersect the activity spaces of potential offenders. The potential targets and victims become actual targets or victims when the potential offender's willingness to commit a crime has been triggered and when the potential target or victim fits the offender's crime template.

Rule 8
The prior rules operate within the built urban form. Crime generators are created by high flows of people through and to nodal activity points. Crime attractors are created when targets are located at nodal activity points of individuals who have a greater willingness to commit crimes.

## CANTER'S MARAUDER AND COMMUTER MODELS

Professor David Canter's approach to geographic profiling focusses on the circle theory of environmental range. In 1993, Canter and Larkin developed two models of offender behavior: marauder and commuter models. Each of these types of crime has its own characteristics and describes the behavior of an offender in a different way (Laukkanen and Santtila, 2006).

Marauder Crimes are committed by static, localized or geographically stable serial offenders who commit crime within a confined area. They are bounded by psychological barriers and landscape features and operate within their awareness space. They are likely to have an anchor point (the haven) from which to operate. The criminal's haven lies within the distribution of crime sites.

Commuter Crimes are committed by mobile dispersed or geographically transient serial offenders who commit crimes over large areas. They have cross cultural and psychological boundaries. Most offences occur outside the offender's awareness space and involve complex hunting strategies. The hunting area tends to lack a definable anchor point.

The distinction between marauders and commuters arose originally from Canter and Larkin's (1993) model of the spatial behavior of criminals during the execution of serial offences. Known as the Circle Theory of Environmental Range the model depicts criminal spatial behavior as bearing a meaningful relationship to the criminal's home base or place of residence. During both criminal and non-criminal movement from the home base, criminals gain an awareness of their environment and subsequently utilize this information in order to identify potential targets.

In his book *Profiling and Serial Crime: Theoretical and Practical Issues* (2014) Wayne Petherick highlights certain limitations with the Canter Larkin 1993 model. He points out that there was no support for a commuter model in a sample of 45 sexual assaulters, but in 41 of the 45 cases, the offender's home was located within the circle. Because of this Canter and Larkin suggested that "there is strong support for the marauder hypothesis as being the most applicable to these sets of offenders."

Petherick goes on to say:

> **Although the theory seems plausible and attractive, there are a number of issues with the model. First, although Canter and Larkin (1993) identified 87% of offenders as marauders, the decision regarding whether one is dealing with a marauder or a commuter when the**

**offender's home base is not known may still be a matter of luck or educated guess.**

If the profiler relies on the statistical probability that the offender is a marauder, then the same general cautions apply as those for any inductive method, such as whether the case is statistically anomalous (in the Canter and Larkin study this would mean that the offender was part of the 13%, or perhaps that the research did not apply in any meaningful way in this community or jurisdiction).

In addition, Petherick raises the following possible limitations:

1. The base is not at the center of the circle of crimes. Accordingly, this will impact on search areas and population numbers in densely populated areas.

2. The eccentricity of the model is important because it may reflect some developmental processes on the criminal's part, whereby he travels further from home in order to commit a crime than at other times.

3. Consequently, the differences between marauding and commuting could possibly be explained by increasing criminal skill or confidence.

4. The representation of ranges using circles is oversimplified. Other research has suggested that in America city expansion from downtown areas may be better indicated by elliptical or sectoral patterns.

5. The number of offenses per offender in the study was relatively small.

6. It is possible that the information used in the modelling did not accurately represent all the crimes committed by the criminals.

## GEOGRAPHICAL TOOLS AND SOFTWARE

Geographic Profilers often employ tools such as Predator, Rigel®, CrimeStat, Dragnet and Gemini to perform geographic analysis. System inputs are crime location addresses or coordinates, often entered through a geographic information system (GIS).

Output is a jeopardy surface (three-dimensional probability surface) or color geoprofile, which depicts the most likely areas of offender residence or search base. These programs assist crime analysts and investigators to focus their resources more effectively by highlighting the crucial geographic areas.

**PREDATOR**
Dr. Grover M. Godwin from the Justice Center at the University of Alaska is the author of *Hunting Serial Predators* (2007). His work offers a unique multivariate analysis approach to profiling. He has developed his own computer system for geographic profiling called Predator. He believes that geographic profiling is more scientific and more accurate than the inferential methods used by the FBI.

According to Godwin, the steps in developing a geographical profile first involve deciding on which of two different ideological positions you will take; the sole use of body dump sites or the use of both the body dump sites and victims' abduction locations or where last seen.

He conducted research with David Canter on fifty-four American serial killers. From this study he believes that the abduction sites significantly affect the predictive power of a program when determining the offender's home base area. Because of this he prefers the second option. This involves gathering more data, but it also ensures that the analysis is more solid.

According to Godwin:

> **The site where the victim was last seen can be developed from any number of sources, such as eyewitness accounts, visual sightings, telephone conversations, and official documents like traffic citations, police field reports, jail booking logs, long distance calls, toll records, and credit card receipts.**

Once he has gathered this information he then seeks to determine the geographical coordinates of both the location where a body was found and the physical address of where the victim was last seen or from which they were abducted. Godwin believes that the best measures are made by visiting all crime locations and obtaining geographical coordinates with a global position unit (GBS).

He then enters the data into Predator. The program produces the same type of 3-D map as Rossmo's Rigel® system, displaying various colors that depict different results.

For example, in the Predator program, a light-colored area suggests a high probability of the offender living in that area, while darker color areas suggests a low probability.

Godwin's primary objective is to provide a psychological theory about the spatial behavior of a certain offender, that is, what caused the offender to travel the way he did, based on data about how killers interact with their victims. Godwin's theories were cemented in 1996 when they were used in a serial murder case in North Carolina.

He had read about the crimes in a Raleigh newspaper and fed whatever facts he could find into his database, which at the time consisted of information from over seven hundred victims. Although the police were skeptical that the murders were connected, Godwin could prove clear links. All the victims were black women who were choked and beaten to death. The geographical pattern indicated a relatively small area of operation, mostly around railroad tracks.

Godwin provided a profile of the offender. He said that the offender was an explosive person between 28 and 35 who would commit his acts in an unplanned but stylized burst of violence. He also provided his opinion of the offender's place of residence.

The day Godwin presented his profile, John Williams, Jr. was arrested for one of the crimes. He soon became a suspect in the others, as well as in five rapes. It later transpired that Godwin was correct in his overall assessment, but most particularly in the geographic pattern as a clue to the offender's home. He says:

> **In the John Williams, Jr. case I predicted within one block where he lived which is more accurate than any other geographical profiling system. Killers have a certain kind of place in mind, where experience has taught them that suitable victims can be found.**

Each subsequent trip to these locations forms something of an analogy with previous successes, modified by experience and perhaps intelligence gained from previous murders. The killer's perception will be shaped both by actual characteristics and those inferred from factors such as where a victim hangs out and with whom.

Then the killer tends to go about his routine activities until the opportunity arises to snatch someone. He may have a passing conversation with the potential victim, see her from afar, or even work with her.

The situational context within which network interactions occur is critical to understanding the hunting patterns of a predator. For example, if the killer targets victims in a location at which contact is likely to be witnessed, the chance of detection will increase.

The significance of this is that by studying potential settings where a victim may have had contact with a killer it can help to narrow the focus of an investigation to promising areas for locating witnesses and for people who may have escaped an abduction attempt.

For Godwin, the areas of greatest risk from serial killers include:

Urban subcultures like pubs, night clubs, and red light areas;
Isolated landscapes such as parking sites, jogging paths, and rest areas;
Areas with a high concentration of elderly people and the poor;
Derelict areas of a city; and, finally
University campuses.

These landscape layouts provide the serial killer with ease of access and escape routes to avoid detection. For example, of the five high-risk victim-targeting areas, the university campus appears to be a safe place.

However, university campuses have certain landscape features, such as large isolated parking lots, which make them ideal for hunting and abducting victims. Ted Bundy is a classic example of an offender who targeted victims on college campuses.

Godwin believes that the places where criminals shop, eat, and get involved in recreation play a significant role in defining their crime awareness space.

## DRAGNET

Dragnet is a geographical prioritization package, developed at the Centre of Investigative Psychology at the University of Liverpool in England. It is based extensively on empirical research into the spatial behavior of offending populations.

Using a series of crime locations, Dragnet prioritizes the surrounding area in order to determine the most likely region or regions for the perpetrators home or base. The use of the term prioritize is very important in this context.

The end result of the Dragnet analysis is a map of several areas. It is not an "X marks the spot" program.

Dragnet is the end result of a series of tests on offence series of serious serial offenders. In a sample of solved 79 US serial killers the percentage of the original search area that had to be searched before the home base of the offender was identified.

For 87% of the sample the offenders home base was identified by searching up to 25% of the search area, for 51% of the sample a search area of only 5% was required. Moreover a search of only 1% of the original search area were required for 15% of the sample.

In a real life situation the search costs would actually be smaller because the Dragnet analysis works with abstract offence series maps containing only the locations of the crime scenes. Accordingly, spaces such as parks and lakes will be included in the prioritized map even though the chances of the offender being based there are minimal.

It is at this stage that local police will contribute their valuable insight into the crime series and its setting to provide a powerful investigative support tool.

There are various stages involved in the analysis. The first is for the user to input the locations of the crimes. This produces an offence map with each black point on the map representing a crime scene. The user then runs the analysis to produce a prioritized map.

The actual formation of the map can indicate additional offence details such as the existence of more than one geographical focus present within the offences possibly indicating the existence of more than one offender.

Dragnet also has features that will adjust the prioritization pattern for city block networks. This option can be used to indicate any linear structuring that exists within an offence series. The results (the line) can then be used with local knowledge of transport networks and case specific information such as time of offence to produce proactive policing strategies.

The software is useful not only as an operational tool for the police but is also invaluable for research into offenders' offence site selection behaviors as well as for other human geographic practices.

## CRIMESTAT

CrimeStat is a Windows based crime mapping software program that conducts spatial and statistical analysis and is designed to interface with a geographic information system (GIS). The program is developed by Ned Levine & Associates, with funding by the National Institute of Justice (NIJ), an agency of the United States Department of Justice.

The program performs spatial analysis on objects located in a GIS. The objects can be points for example, events, locations, or zones like blocks, traffic analysis zones, cities or lines like street segments. The program can analyze the distribution of the objects, identify hot spots, indicate spatial autocorrelation, monitor the interaction of events in space and time, and model travel behavior. While some of its tools are specific to crime analysis, others can be applied in many fields. There are 55 statistical routines in the program.

CrimeStat was developed in the mid-1990s. The first prototype was a Unix-based C++ program called Pointstat. It was developed to analyze motor vehicle crashes in Honolulu. Then in 1996, the National Institute of Justice funded the first version of CrimeStat and the early Pointstat routines were folded into the program. It was first released in August 1999. The latest version was designed in July 2010.

CrimeStat can input data both attribute and GIS files but requires that all datasets have geographical coordinates assigned for the objects. CrimeStat uses three coordinate systems: spherical (longitude, latitude), projected and directional (angles).

Unlike some other spatial statistics programs, CrimeStat has no mapping capabilities and must be used with GIS software. Because CrimeStat analyzes points in most routines, its results are not always consistent with those of software that analyzes areas like GeoDa.

## RIGEL®

Rigel® is Rossmo's model which we have already discussed. Rossmo extended the work of the Brentinghams and developed a "criminal geographic targeting" algorithm, which was later patented and incorporated into the Rigel® software application. Levine (2002, p. 357) indicates that the journey-to-crime routines in CrimeStat "builds on the Rossmo framework, but extends its modeling capability."

But while Rigel®, CrimeStat, and Dragnet are based on different types of distance-decay functions, they produce the same general type of output.

In contrast to a single spatial mean which was used by Stuart Kind in the *Yorkshire Ripper* case, these software applications create a grid over an area and then calculate the probability that the offender's base of operations is in each grid cell based on the specified crime-related.

As Harries (1999) points out, law enforcement officials could use this information for:

(a) suspect and tip prioritization;

(b) address-based searches of police record systems;

(c) patrol saturation and surveillance;

(d) canvasses and searches;

(e) mass DNA screening prioritization;

(f) department of motor vehicle searches;

(g) zip code prioritization; and

(h) information request mail-outs.

## ASSESSMENT OF GEOGRAPHICAL PROFILING

No one can deny that the advent of geographic profiling represents an important step in moving computerized crime mapping beyond static displays of crime locations and toward more analytical mapping that, in turn, help analysts interpret spatial data.

In recent years this type of profiling has received considerable media attention. The Washington, DC area sniper case, in particular, led to several media stories on geographic profiling (Bowman, 2002; Lewis, 2002; Onion, 2002). It even resulted in an appearance by Kim Rossmo on ABC-TV's *Good Morning America.*

Geographical profiling had resulted in solving several high profile cases in America, Canada and Britain. But, despite its recently found celebrity status just how effective is it?

One of the difficulties in evaluating the approach is that there has not been a thorough evaluation of any of the geographic profiling software applications. No one really knows if any one is better than the other.

There is no independent source available to help law enforcement agencies decide on the acquisition of a geographic profiling software best suited to their own individual needs.

Everyone is aware that geographical profiling does not "solve" murder or rape cases or any other types of crime for that matter. Rather, the method provides an additional avenue of scientific investigation that, with the many other forensic specialties, may assist the investigation of serial crime.

But while it is a useful tool for assisting investigations, like any other models there are certain limitations. One of the criticisms often levied against it is that it only considers the spatial behavior of serial offenders. It may not distinguish between multiple offenders operating in the same area and following similar *modi operandi.*

According to Brent Turvey, author of *Criminal Profiling,* geographical profiling, like trait analysis or future crime prediction, relies too strongly on a single manifestation of behavior, for example, offense location selection, and attempts to infer meaning from the overall emotional context.

Brent believes that geographical profiling cannot then distinguish between two similar offenders operating in the same area and may mistakenly assign crimes to the wrong person. It's a valid point. He also believes it only works when the offender actually lives in or near his circle of offenses.

Like all computer programs the systems are really only as good as the data fed into them. They cannot analyze all the information involved in a crime series and they are only as good as the accuracy of their algorithms' underlying assumptions.

In order for the programs to be effective they require accurate data on the offences that have been committed in an area. As we have previously seen, police data on crime is limited by a number of factors that lead to under-reporting, so the data from which crime maps are generated can often be incomplete. Additional problems can arise from inconsistencies in how the locations of crimes may be recorded by the police.

Problems also arise from the vast amount of data that the police might have available. It can sometimes be difficult to know what to input and what to leave out when attempting to construct a crime map. The fact is that while geographical profiling involves objective measures, it still relies on subjective interpretation, which makes it subject to the interpreter's experience and skill.

Canter (2003) suggests that it is of most potential use in countries like the United States where there are many different law enforcement agencies, possibly with little data sharing between them. There, geographical profiling using data from different sources can link crimes that otherwise might not have been linked.

Despite the criticism, geographical profiling has much to offer law enforcement. It is of considerable value in helping them determine how to deploy resources; how to narrow down the area in which door-to-door canvassing can be undertaken; it allows informed judgments to be made about which crimes are linked; it can help prioritize suspects; it can develop strategies for linkage analysis of information and even help to make up an effective polygraph session with a suspect. In the form pioneered by David Canter and his colleagues, it is also based on well-established psychological principles and conducted in a scientific manner: hypotheses are developed which can be tested against evidence and modified or rejected as the evidence dictates.

At the moment this approach of profiling is endorsed more firmly in Canada than in America. As of 1997, the Royal Canadian Mounted Police put in place Rossmo's Rigel® program. They plan to use this to complement their Violent Criminal Linkage Analysis System (ViCLAS) so they can conduct automated computer searches and carry out efficient case management. The approach is also rapidly gaining support in America and Britain. And for some, geographical profiling is the way of the future.

# 6 EPILOGUE

*The criminal is the creative artist; the detective only the critic.*

**G.K. Chesterton, *The Blue Cross: A Father Brown Mystery* (1910)**

## WHAT IS CRIMINAL PROFILING?

Essentially, criminal profiling is a system used to help find suspects involving forensic, physical and behavioral evidence.

Copson (1996) described offender profiling as a "term of convenience". By this he meant that a technique is used to discover inferences about the behavior of an offender and to draw conclusions about the type of person the offender is.

Turco (1993) described offender profiling as "the preparation of a biographical 'sketch' gathered from information taken at a crime scene, from the personal history and habits of a victim, and integrating this with known psychological theory."

So, they construct a 'sketch' or "profile" which can be used by the police to help them with their enquiry. Criminal profiling is different from 'clues' left at the scene, such as blood, hair, semen, and saliva, in that it provides the police with less visible clues at the crime scene, clues like the choice of victim, location, type of assault, and anything said or not said to the victim.

## THE AIM OF PROFILING

The overall aim is to help the police to narrow the field of investigation. The profiler is helping to put a personality to the offender and his motivations for committing the crime.

Holmes (1989) suggests that profiling is most useful when the crime scene reflects psychopathology, like sadistic assaults and 90 per cent of profiling attempts involve murder or rape.

## THE APPROACHES

Ainsworth (2001) identified four main approaches to criminal profiling:

The geographical approach. This approach examines the patterns in the location and timing of offences to make judgments about links between crimes and suggestions about where offenders live and work.

The investigative psychology approach developed out of geographical profiling and uses established psychological theories and methods of analysis to predict offender characteristics from offending behavior.

The typological approach, often called the crime scene analysis approach, which is used extensively by the FBI, involves looking at the characteristics of crime scenes to assign offenders to different categories, each category of offender having different typical characteristics.

The clinical approach, sometimes called the diagnostic evaluation approach. This approach uses insights from psychiatry and clinical psychology to aid investigation where an offender is thought to be suffering from a mental illness of other psychological abnormality.

There is considerable debate about which of these approaches is the most effective way of profiling offenders and, indeed, whether psychological profiling really has anything useful to offer crime detection at all.

But, theoretically, while there are four separate approaches to criminal profiling, essentially, there are really just two approaches to profiling; the American approach and the British approach. Geographical profiling is regarded as a sub-type of investigative psychology.

## EVALUATION

The chief arguments against profiling, in simple terms are as follows:

1. All profiles are generalizations that do not accommodate individual differences. There is a risk that these generalizations come from inappropriate samples.

2. The information on which these theories are based come from known criminals who have been caught. Not only is there the difficulty that most serial killers are pathological liars but even more importantly, there is a whole section of the criminal population, that is, successful criminals who have not been caught, whose data is completely absent.

3. There are dangers, already proven, that inaccurate profiles can cause the wrong person to be convicted.

## BOTTOM UP V TOP DOWN APPROACHES

Bottom-up processing is where information is gathered and conclusions are drawn strictly from the evidence. Previous knowledge and information is ignored.

Boon and Davies (1992) suggest that the British approach to criminal profiling is a bottom-up approach because it involves working with detailed information gathered from the scene of the crime as well as from information about the crime. From this detailed information investigators are able to draw up a profile of the offender.

So, it uses details from the crime scene in order to gradually build up a clearer picture of what characteristics the offender is likely to exhibit, in terms of how they socialize, where they live and work, and what demographic they're likely to be part of. It's an important part of making a case as it gives the police a starting point for narrowing down suspects and providing a second opinion. Copson (1995) found that detectives often cited that offender profiling helps to support their suspicions of suspects.

The reasoning involved here is inductive, because any conclusions are merely tentative, being formed as they are from what has been observed. The conclusion can be altered from any change in what is observed or any additional information that comes to hand. The 1992 case of Rachel Nickell involving psychologist Paul Britton (pictured below) is an example of the British bottom-up approach.

Whilst walking her two-year-old son on Wimbledon Common, Rachel Nickell was stabbed forty nine times in front of her son. Profiler Paul Britton prepared a psychological profile for the police. A suspect called Colin Stagg fitted the profile. However, there was little or no evidence connecting Mr. Stagg to the case. Working with Britton, a female officer went undercover and got to know Stagg in the hope of extracting evidence from him. Stagg was arrested.

However, the trial showed many inconsistencies. For example, Stagg knew the location of the crime but said, incorrectly, that Rachel Nickell had been raped. These inconsistencies had been ignored by the police who were sure that the profiling had led them to the offender. The female police officer later resigned from her job while Britton was heavily criticized. He was charged with misconduct.

In October 2002 all charges of professional misconduct against him were dismissed. Britton, often described as the real-life version of television's *Cracker*, faced seven charges of misconduct after the Metropolitan Police asked for his help in catching the killer in the Rachel Nickell case. But after a two-day hearing, the British Psychological Society disciplinary committee concluded Mr Britton's work on the 1992 murder inquiry could not be properly investigated. The committee ruled he could not get a fair hearing.

The case against Stagg collapsed in 1994 when the main plank of the prosecution's case, an exchange of letters with a policewoman posing as a pen-pal, was ruled inadmissible. The policewoman, who was given the pseudonym Lizzie James in court, had encouraged Mr Stagg to swap violent fantasies in an effort to get him to admit to the crime. Britton, who helped in the Fred West and James Bulger murder inquiries and is still used as an expert witness in trials, concluded Mr Stagg had the same "sexually deviant-based personality disorder" as the killer during the original investigation.

The disciplinary hearing was told Mr Britton allegedly "pulled the strings" while helping the police investigation. The committee heard he was "totally discredited" after the case and had broken British Psychology Society's rules.

Turvey (1999) concludes that this is an example of profiling being taken too far.

Gudjonsson and Haward (1998) outline another example in the John Torney case. In this case an RUC police officer from Cookstown, County Tyrone, Northern Ireland was convicted of the slaughter of his wife, son and daughter in 1994. Torney claimed his fourteen year old son killed his wife and sister and then turned the gun on himself. The Crown argued he was lying and had killed his family. The jury believed the prosecution and he was convicted, dying two years later in prison from a heart attack.

On the 20 September 1994 Torney called his local Cookstown RUC Station and told a colleague: "Sam, get the police here immediately to my house. The young boy's gone clean, fucking mad." Three officers went into the bungalow and found 13-year-old John junior dead in his bedroom with a bullet wound to his head. He was wearing black, police issue gloves, and his father's Ruger revolver lay at his side. In an adjoining room lay 11-year-old Emma. She was dead and had been shot in the head.

Torney's wife, Linda, was found lying in the master bedroom. She had also been shot in the head, and officers heard her groaning; but as they tried to save her, she died. The gloves found on John junior were contaminated with firearm residue. John Torney senior's defence team argue that if he had worn the gloves during the shootings and then placed them on his son's hands it would have been impossible to do this without transferring residue onto the boy's hands.

Yet when John junior's hands were tested they were clean. John Torney senior had small amounts of firearm residue on him. The Crown believed he washed himself after the shootings. At the trial profiling evidence suggested that the killings had been executed calmly and efficiently by someone conversant with firearms and ballistics and that this simply did not tie in with the argument that the son had "gone berserk." It was more likely that Torney Senior had committed the murders. The jury accepted this argument on a ten to two majority. The case is now subject to a review.

David Canter uses the inductive profiling model. This model is based on statistical analysis and use of probabilities, in which information from previous crimes is used to form an empirical base (from actual evidence) or the development of hypotheses. This approach is based on applying psychological theory to show how and why variations in criminal behavior occur and pointing out the consistencies within the action of offenders.

Canter (1989) suggests that criminal behavior may provide clues to other aspects of the criminal's everyday life. For example, a profile is built on three assumptions:

Firstly, offenders tend to demonstrate interpersonal coherence. So, if the crime is violent, this pattern of behavior may very well reflect the way the offender treats people in everyday life. Therefore the type of victim and how he or she is treated may indicate something about their offender.

Secondly, the time and place of the crime may have significance. Canter was one of the first to introduce geographical profiling in Britain, which takes into account an individual's spatial behavior and helps to predict the offender's residence based on the location of the crimes he commits, such as the sites where victims' bodies are dumped and abduction sites.

Thirdly, many criminals today demonstrate forensic awareness: if police have previously questioned criminals for something similar, they need to check police records carefully. Attempts to destroy evidence suggest that the person has previous convictions.

By contrast, top-down processing involves using previous knowledge and information to draw conclusions about a current situation. Previously stored knowledge is used to make judgments. America adopts the top-down processing approach. In 1979 the FBI began collecting data from interviews of convicted serial killers and murderers. From these interviews they constructed a profile of the type of person likely to commit such crimes. It was thought, for example, that sex killers were more likely to be white, male and unmarried, from dysfunctional families, unemployed or have unskilled jobs and suffer from alcohol and psychiatric problems.

The American approach is referred to as a top-down approach because it involves going from previously known information to a conclusion about the offender. The approach is based on data collected from interviews with known criminals who have been caught. From such interviews, and using the experience of those involved in crimes, a classification system (for example, classifying murders are organized or disorganized) is built up which forms the basis for drawing up profiles.

The profiling procedure has four stages:

Firstly, as much information as possible is collected from as many sources as possible.

Secondly, the crime is categorized as organized or disorganized.

Thirdly, hypotheses are developed about the behavior of the victims and of the criminal.

Fourthly, the profile is generated to include details of physical appearance and demographic characteristics, for example, the age and race of the offender, his habits and personality.

This type of profiling is useful for crimes such as rape and arson, and killings that involve extreme practices.

In the past, offender profiling in America used to rely almost exclusively on the behavioral analysis of crime scenes and information obtained from victims and other witnesses. Physical and behavioral evidence within a series of crimes or from similar crimes would be examined and in this way previous knowledge would be used to construct a set of characteristics belonging to the offender.

The American approach is referred to as a top-down approach because of the use of previous experience. However, today the approach tends to be less rigid. Profiling is now more likely to include intuition and investigative experience.

To repeat then, the British approach starts with all the available evidence and then looks for links and associations, whereas the American approach tries to place the crime into the classification system, that is, disorganized or organized. Remember, profiling does not identify the offender (although it can.) It's purpose is to narrow the field of the investigation and suggest the type of person who committed the crime.

## PSYCHOLOGICAL THEORY V TYPOLOGY BASED ON EXPERIENCE

The bottom up approach is based on psychological theory, as opposed to the top down approach which uses typology based on experience. One particularly prominent theory used when creating an offender profile is Canter's criminal consistency hypothesis.

By this Canter says that people tend to behave consistently, and thus the criminal is likely to behave at the crime scene in a similar way to in their normal life.

The theory consists of two parts:

1. interpersonal consistency; and,

2. spatial consistency.

Interpersonal consistency refers to how the criminal acts towards the victim (if there is one). For example, if a female victim was raped and physically abused, it could be that the offender has been in or is currently in an abusive relationship, or that they show no respect to females they come into contact with on a daily basis, such as colleagues or family members.

Spatial consistency works on the basis that criminals are likely to commit a crime in a location they feel comfortable. This might be en-route to a friend's house or their workplace. If it's in an urban location for example, they may also live in a similar area close by. Thus, as it looks for patterns, this approach is considered to be quantitative.

## SIMILARITIES AND DIFFERENCES

Even within both approaches there are differences. In the British model Paul Britton analyses information from the scene and likely behavior patterns from the offender. Unlike Canter, he doesn't seem to focus much on statistics although Canter also works within the "bottom-up approach." Canter uses information from past crimes and this can be construed as a "top-down approach" in so far as it uses past experiences. However, Canter mainly uses information from the crimes under investigation, and collates information from many different sources, "bottom-up" and empirical.

The American emphasis on "top-down" processing does involve using past experience, and focuses on what has previously been learned. But Canter's main criticism of the American approach is that relying on interviews with criminals has got to be unreliable. However, the American approach also uses information from the crime scene.

## INDUCTIVE V DEDUCTIVE

Inductive reasoning refers to information from the environment and many other sources that is weighed up, and from which conclusions are drawn. Inductive criminal profiling uses statistics, especially correlations, in order to see whether there are shared characteristics between crimes. Generalizations are then made. The statistics tend to come from those who have already been convicted of crimes.

Deductive reasoning is logical reasoning. It tends to be more definite than inductive reasoning. In deductive criminal profiling if the first statement is true, then the conclusion is also true. For example, Turvey (1999):

> **The situation is that the offender disposed of a victim's body in a remote area and tire tracks were found at the scene. The profiler could say 'if the tire tracks belong to the offender, then the offender has access to a vehicle and can drive'.**

# 7 BIBLIOGRAPHY & REFERENCES

ACPO. (2006). *Murder investigation manual.* Wyboston: National Centre for Policing Excellence.

Ahadi, S., & Diener, E. (1989). Multiple determinants and effect size. *Journal of Personality and Social Psychology, 56*

Ainsworth, P. B. (2001). *Offender profiling and crime analysis.* Devon: Willan Publishing.

Alison, L., Bennell, C., Mokros, A., & Ormerod, D. (2002). The personality paradox in offender profiling: A theoretical review of the processes involved in deriving background characteristics from crime scene actions. *Psychology, Public Policy and Law, 8*

Alison, L., & Canter, D. (1999). *Profiling in policy and practice.* Dartmouth: Aldershot.

Alison, L., Goodwill, A., Almond, L., van den Heuvel, C., & Winter, J. (2010). Pragmatic solutions to offender profiling and behavioural investigative advice. *Legal and Criminological Psychology*

Alison, L., McLean, C., & Almond, L. (2007). Profiling suspects. In: T. Newburn, T. Williamson, & A. Wright (Eds.). *Handbook of Criminal Investigation.* Devon: Willan.

Alison, L., Smith, M. D., Eastman, O., & Rainbow, L. (2003). Toulimn's philosophy of argument and its relevance to offender profiling. *Psychology, Crime, and Law, 9*

Alison, L., Smith, M. D., & Morgan, K. (2003). Interpreting the accuracy of offender profiles. *Psychology, Crime, & Law, 9*

Alison, L., West, A., & Goodwill, A. (2004). The Academic and the Practitioner: Pragmatists' views of Offender Profiling. *Psychology, Public Policy and Law, 10*

Atilt, R.L. & Reese, J.T. (1980) 'A psychological assessment of crime profiling', *FBI Law Enforcement Bulletin*, 49(3), 22-25.

Arrigo, B.A., & Purcell, C.E. (2001). Explaining paraphilias and lust murder: Toward an integrated model. *International Journal of Offender Therapy and Comparative Criminology, 45*

Ault, R., & Reese, J. (1980). A psychological assessment of crime: Profiling. *FBI Law Enforcement Bulletin , 49*

Beauregard, E. (2010). Rape and sexual assault in investigative psychology: The contribution of sex offenders' research. *Journal of Investigative Psychology and Offender Profiling, 7*

Beauregard, E., & Field, J. (2008). Body disposal patterns of sexual murderers: Implications for Offender Profiling. *Journal of Police and Criminal Psychology, 23*

Beauregard, E., Proulx, J., Rossmo, K., Leclerc, B., & Allaire, J.F. (2007). Script analysis of the hunting process of serial sex offenders. *Criminal Justice and Behavior, 34*

Beck J.P., O'Sullivan, B.J. & Ogilvie, A.B. (1989) An Australian Violent Criminal Apprehension Programme: A Feasibility Study, National Police Research Unit, Adelaide.

Bennell, C., & Canter, D. (2002). Linking commercial burglaries by modus operandi: Tests using regression and ROC analysis. *Science & Justice, 42*

Bennell, C., & Jones, N. (2005). Between a ROC and a hard place. *International Journal of Investigative Psychology and Offender Profiling, 2*

Bennel, C., Jones, N., Taylor, P., & Snook, B. (2006). Validities and abilities in criminal profiling: A critique of the studies conducted by Richard Kocsis and his colleagues. *International Journal of Offender Therapy and Comparative Criminology, 50*

Blackburn, R. (1993) *The Psychology of Criminal Conduct,* John Wiley & Sons, Liverpool.

Blau, T. H. (1994). *Psychological services for law enforcement.* New York: Wiley.

Boon, J. (1997). The contribution of personality theories to psychological profiling. In J.L. Jackson, & D.A. Bekerian (Eds). *Offender profiling: Theory, research, and practice* (pp. 44-59). Hoboken, NJ: John Wiley & Sons Inc.

Brentingham, P. L., & Brentingham P. J. (1981). Notes on the Geometry of Crime. In P. J. Brentingham, & P. L Brentingham (Eds.), *Environmental Criminology* (pp. 27-54). Beverley Hills: Sage Publications.

Britton, P. (1997). *The jigsaw man.* Reading, England: Bantam Press.

Brussel, J. (1968) *Casebook of a Criminal Psychiatrist,* Bernard Gels, New York.

Burgess, A.W., Hartman, C.R., Ressler, R.K., Douglas J.E. & McCormack, A. (1986) 'Sexual homicide: a motivational model', *Journal of Interpersonal Violence,* 1 (3), 251-72.

Callcott, G. (1990) Criminal profiles, *Police Life,* October, 8.

Canter, D. (1989). Offender profiling, *The Psychologist, 2,* 12-16.

Canter, D. (1994). *Criminal shadows.* London: Harper Collins.

Canter, D. (1995). Psychology of offender profiling. In R. Bull & D. Carson (Eds.), *Handbook of psychology in legal contexts* (pp. 343-355). Chichester, UK: John Wiley and Sons.

Canter, D. (2004). Offender profiling and investigative psychology. *Journal of Investigative Psychology and Offender Profiling, 1*, 1-15.

Canter, D. (2011). Resolving the offender "profiling equations" and the emergence of an investigative psychology. *Current Directions in Psychological Sciences, 20,* 293-320.
Canter, D., Alison, L., Alison, E., & Wentink, N. (2004). The organized/disorganized typology of serial murder. *Psychology, Public Policy and Law, 10*, 293-320.

Canter, D.V., Bennell, C., Alison, L.J., & Reddy, S. (2003). Differentiating sex offences: A behaviorally based thematic classification of stranger rapes. *Behavioral Sciences and the Law, 21*, 157-174.

Canter, D.V., & Heritage, R. (1990). A multivariate model of sexual offence behavior: Developments in 'offender profiling'. *The Journal of Forensic Psychiatry, 1*, 185- 212.

Canter, D.V., & Wentink, N. (2004). An empirical test of Holmes and Holmes's serial murder typology. *Criminal Justice and Behavior, 31*, 489-515.

Canter, D., Heritage, R., Wilson, M., Davies, A., Kirby, S., Holden, R., et al. (1991). *A facet approach to offender profiling: Vol. 1.* Guilford, England: University of Surrey, Psychology Department.

Canter, D., Hughes, D., & Kirby, S. (1998). Paedophilia: pathology, criminality, or both? The development of a multivariate model of offence behaviour in child sexual abuse. *The Journal of Forensic Psychiatry, 9,* 532-555.

Canter, D. (2004). Geographic Profiling of Criminals. *Medico-legal Journal,* 72, 53- 66.

Canter, D. (2005). Confusing Operational Predicaments and Cognitive Explorations: Comments on Rossmo and Snook et al. *Applied Cognitive Psychology,* 19(5), 663-668.

Canter, D., Coffey, T., Huntley, M., & Missen, C. (2000). Predicting Serial Killers' Home Base Using a Decision Support System. *Journal of Quantitative Criminology,* 16, 457-478.

Canter, D. V., & Gregory, A. (1994). Identifying the Residential Location of Rapists. *Journal of the Forensic Science Society,* 34, 169-175.

Canter, D. & Hammond, L. (2006). A comparison of the efficacy of different decay functions in geographical profiling for a sample of US serial killers. *Journal of Investigative Psychology and Offender Profiling,* 3, 91-103.

Canter, D., & Hammond, L. (2007). *Prioritizing Burglars: Comparing the Effectiveness of Geographic Profiling Methods.*

Canter, D., & Hodge, S. (2000). *Criminals' Mental Maps.* In L. S. Turnbull, E. H.

Canter, D., & Larkin, P. (1993). The Environmental Range of Serial Rapists. *Journal of Environmental Psychology,* 13, 63-69.

Canter, D., & Shalev, K. (2000). Putting Crime in its Place: Psychological Process in Crime Site Location. Paper for Wheredunit? Investigating the Role of Place in Crime and Criminality. Crime Mapping Research Center of the NIJ, San Diego.

Canter, D., & Snook, B. (1999). Modelling the Home Location of Serial Offenders. Paper presented at the Third Annual International Crime Mapping Research Conference, Orlando, December.

Catalano, P. (2000). Applying geographical analysis to serial crime investigations to predict the location of future targets and determine offender residence. Unpublished master's thesis, University of Western Australia, Australia.

Clarke, R., & Felson, M. (1993). Routine Activity and Rational Choice. New Brunswick: Transaction Publishers.

Coleman, C., & Norris, C. (2000). *Introducing criminology*. Devon: William Publishing.

Copson, G. (1995). *Coals to Newcastle? Police use of offender profiling*. London: Home Office Police Research Group.

Copson, G., Badcock, R., Boon, J., & Britton, P. (1997). Editorial: Articulating a systematic approach to clinical crime profiling. *Criminal Behaviour and Mental Health, 7*, 13-17.

Costello, A., & Wiles, P. (2001). GIS and the Journey to Crime: An Analysis of Patterns in South Yorkshire. In A. Hirschfield & K. Bowers (Eds.), *Mapping and Analysing Crime Data: Lessons from Research and Practice* (pp. 27-60). London: Taylor and Francis.

Crabbé, A., Decoene, S., & Vertommen, H. (2008). Profiling homicide offenders: A review of assumptions and theories. *Aggression and Violent Behavior, 13*, 88-106.

Davies, A. (1991). The use of DNA profiling and behavioural science in the investigation of sexual offences. *Medicine, Science and Law, 31*, 95-101.

Davies, A. (1999). Criminal personality profiling and crime scene assessment: A contemporary investigative tool to assist law enforcement public safety. *Journal of Contemporary Criminal Justice, 15*, 291-301.

Davies, A. (1994) Editorial: offender profiling, *Medicine, Science and the Law*, 34(3), 185-86.

Davis, J.A. (1994) Criminal investigative analysis: selected readings in criminal and psychological profiling, unpublished paper, San Diego CA.

Davies, A., & Dale, A. (1995). Locating the Stranger Rapist. London Home Office Police Department, Special Interest Series Paper 3.Downs, R. M., & Stea, D. (1973). Cognitive maps and spatial behaviour: Process and products. In R. Downs, & D. Stea (Eds.), *Image and environment* (pp. 8-26). Chicago: Aldine.

Depue, R.L. (1986) 'An American response to an era of violence', FBI Law Enforcement Bulletin, 55(12), 1-8.

Dietz, P.E., Hazelwood, R.R., & Warren, J. (1990). The sexually sadistic criminal and his offenses. *The Bulletin of the American Academy of Psychiatry and the Law, 18*, 163- 178.

Dietz, P.E. (1985) 'Sex offender profiling by the FBI: a preliminary conceptual model', in *Clinical Criminology,* eds M.H. Ben-Aron, S.J. Hucher & C.D. Webster, M & M Graphics, Toronto, 207-19.

Doan, B., & Snook, B. (2008). A failure to find empirical support for the homology assumption in criminal profiling. *Journal of Police and Criminal Psychology, 23,* 61- 70.

Douglas, J., Burgess, A., Burgess, A., & Ressler, R. (1992). *Crime classification manual.* Lexington, MA: Lexington Books.

Douglas, J., Ressler, R., Burgess, A. W., & Hartman, C. (1986). Criminal profiling from crime scene analysis. *Behavioral Sciences & the Law, 4*, 401-421.

Douglas, J.E. & Burgess, A.E. (1986) 'Criminal profiling: a viable investigative tool against violent crime', *FBI Law Enforcement Bulletin,* 55(12), 9-13.

Douglas, J.E. & Munn, C. (1992) 'Violent crime scene analysis: modus operandi, signature and staging', *FBI Law Enforcement Bulletin,* 61 (2), 1-10.

Douglas, J.E. & Olshaker, M. (1996) *Mindhunter,* Heinemann, London.

Dowden, C., Bennell, C., & Bloomfield, S. (2007). Advances in offender profiling: A systematic review of the profiling literature published over the past three decades. *Journal of Police and Criminal Psychology, 22*, 44-56.

Downs, R. M., & Stea, D. (1977). *Maps in Minds*. London: Harper and Row.

Edwards, M. J., & Grace, R. C. (2006). Analysing the offence locations and residential base of serial arsonists in New Zealand. *Australian Psychologist,* 41(3), 219-226.

Egger, S. (1984). A working definition of serial murder and the reduction of linkage blindness. *Journal of Police Science and Administration, 12*, 348-357.

Felman, P. (1993) *The Psychology of Crime,* Cambridge University Press, Cambridge.

Fisher, A.J. (1993) *Techniques of Crime Scene Investigation,* 5th edition, Elsevier, New York.

Fleming, L. (1994) Serial murder, *Australian Police Journal* 48(6), 59-72.

Frank, G. (1966) *The Boston Strangler*, Signet, New York.

Fritzon, K. (2001). An examination of the relationship between distance travelled and motivational aspects of arson. *Journal of Environmental Psychology*, 21, 45-60.

Gabor, T., & Gottheil, E. (1984). Offender Characteristics and Spatial Mobility: An Empirical Study and Some Policy Implications. *Journal of Criminology*, 26, 267-281. Harries, K., & LeBeau, J. (2007).Issues in the Geographic Profiling of Crime: Review and Commentary.

Geberth, V.J. (1981) 'Psychological profiling', *Law and Order*, 46-52.

Geberth, V.J. (1983), *Practical Homicide Investigation*, Elsevier, New York.

Gee, D., & Belofastov, A. (2007). Profiling Sexual Fantasy: Fantasy in Sexual Offending and the Implications for Criminal Profiling. In R. N. Kocsis (Ed.), *Criminal profiling: International theory, research and practice* (pp. 49-71). Totowa, NJ: Humana Press Inc.

Goodwill, A. M., & Alison, L. (2007). When is profiling possible? Offence planning and aggression as moderators in predicting offender age from victim age in stranger rape. *Behavioral Sciences & the Law, 25*, 823-840.

Goodwin, J. (1978) *Murder USA: The Ways We Kill Each Other*, Ballanrine, New York.

Grubin, D., Kelly, P., & Brunsdon, C. (2001). *Linking serious sexual assault through behavior.* London: Home Office, Research Development and Statistics Directorate.

Gudjonsson, G. (1992) *The Psychology of Interrogations, Confessions and Testimony*, John Wiley & Sons, London.

Gudjonsson, G.H., & Copson, G. (1997). The role of the expert in criminal investigation. In J.L. Jackson & D.A. Bekerain (Eds), *Offender profiling: theory, research and practice* (pp. 61-76). West Sussex, England: John Wiley & Sons.

Hagen, M. (1992) 'Special issues in serial homicide', in Homicide: Patterns, Prevention and Control, eds H.
Strang & S.A. Gerull, *Australian Institute of Criminology, Canberra*, 135-37.

Hazelwood, R.R., & Burgess, A.W. (1987). An introduction to the serial rapist research by the FBI. *FBI Law Enforcement Bulletin, 56*, 16-24.

Hazelwood, R.R., Reboussin, R., & Warren, J.I. (1989). Serial rape: Correlates of increased aggression and the relationship of offender pleasure to victim resistance. *Journal of Interpersonal Violence*, *4*, 65–78.

Hazelwood, R.R., Dietz, P.E. & Burgess, A.W. (1982)
Sexual fatalities: behavioural reconstruction in
equivocal cases, *Journal of Forensic Sciences,* 127(4), 763-73.
Hazelwood, R.R. & Douglas, J.E. (1980) The lust
murderer, *FBI Law Enforcement Bulletin*, 49(3), 18-22.

Hazelwood, R., & Warren, J. (2003). Linkage analysis: Modus operandi, ritual and signature in serial sexual crime. *Aggression and Violent Behavior, 8*, 587-598.

Hendrix & B. D. Dent (Eds.), *Atlas of Crime, Mapping the Criminal Landscape* (pp 187-191). Phoenix, Arizona: Oryx Press.

Hicks, S. J., & Sales, B. D. (2006). *Criminal profiling: Developing an effective science and practice.* Washington, D.C.: American Psychological Association.

Holmes, R. M., & De Burger, J. (1988). *Serial murder.* London: Sage Publications.

Holmes, R.M., & Holmes, S.T. (1998). *Serial murder* (2nd ed.). Thousand Oaks, CA: Sage.

Homant, R. J., & Kennedy, D. B. (1998). Psychological aspects of crime scene profiling: Validity research. *Criminal Justice and Behavior, 25*, 319-343.

Home Office (2004). *Offender management caseload statistics 2003. England and Wales December 2004 (Table 8.2).* www.homeoffice.gov.uk/rds/hosb2004.html.

House, J. C. (1997). Towards a practical application of offender profiling: The RNC's criminal suspect prioritization system. In J. L. Jackson & D. A. Bekerain (Eds.), *Offender profiling: Theory, research and practice* (pp. 177-190). Chichester, England: Wiley.

Howlett, J., Hanfland, K., & Ressler R. (1986). Violent Criminal Apprehension Program – VICAP: A progress report. *FBI Law Enforcement Bulletin, 55,* 14-22.

Icove, D.J. & Estepp, M.H. (1987) Motive based offender profiles of arson and fire related crimes, *FBI Law Enforcement Bulletin* 56(9), 17-23.

Jackson, J., Van Hoppen, P.J. & Hebrink, J. (1993) Does the Service Meet the Needs? *Netherlands Institute for the Study of Criminality*, Amsterdam.

Jeffers, H.P. (1992) *Profiles in Evil*, Warner Brothers, London.

Jackson, J. L., van de Eshof, P., & de Kleuver, E. E. (1997). A research approach to offender profiling. In J. L. Jackson & D. A. Bekerain (Eds.), *Offender profiling: theory practice and research* (pp. 107-132). Chichester: Wiley & Sons Ltd.

Jackson, J. L., van Koppen, P. J., & Herbrink, J. C. M. (1993). *Does the service meet the needs? An evaluation of consumer satisfaction with specific profile analysis and investigative advice as offered by the Scientific Research Advisory Unit of the National Criminal Intelligence Division (CRI).* The Netherlands: Netherlands Institute for the Study of Criminality and Law Enforcement (NISCALE).

Jankowski, D. (2002). *A beginner's guide to the MCMI-III.* Washington, DC: American Psychological Association.

Keppel, R. D., & Walter, R. (1999). Profiling killers: A revised classification model for understanding sexual murder. *International Journal of Offender Therapy and Comparative Criminology, 43*, 417-437.

Kind, S. (1987). Navigational Ideas and the Yorkshire Ripper Investigation. *Journal of Navigation,* 40, 385-393.

Knight, R. A., Warren, J. I., Reboussin, R., & Soley, B. (1998). Predicting rapist type from crime-scene variables. *Criminal Justice and Behavior, 25*, 46-80.

Kocsis, R. (1995) Offender personality profiling: a viable investigative supplement, unpublished paper, Bond University.

Kocsis, R. (1996) Criminal personality profiling: features of arson in Australia, MA Criminology Thesis, Bond University.

Kocsis, R.N. (2003). Criminal psychological profiling: Validities and abilities. *International Journal of Offender Therapy and Comparative Criminology*, *47*, 126-144.

Kocsis, R. N. (2004). Psychological profiling of serial arson offenses: An assessment of skills and accuracy. *Criminal Justice and Behavior, 31*, 341-361.

Kocsis, R.N., Cooksey, R.W., & Irwin, H.J. (2002). Psychological profiling of offender characteristics from crime behaviors in serial rape offences. *International Journal of Offender Therapy and Comparative Criminology, 46*, 144-169.

Kocsis, R.N., & Irwin, H.J. (1997). An analysis of spatial patterns in serial rape, arson and burglary: The utility of Circle Theory of environmental range to psychological profiling. *Psychiatry, Psychology and Law*, *4*, 195–206.

Kocsis, R. N., Irwin, H. J., & Hayes, A. F. (1998). Organised and disorganised criminal behaviour syndromes in arsonists: A validation study of a psychological profiling concept. Australian and New Zealand Journal of Psychiatry, Psychology, and Law, 5, *117-131.*

Kocsis, R. N., Irwin, H. J., Hayes, A. F., & Nunn, R. (2000). Expertise in psychological profiling: A comparative assessment. *Journal of Interpersonal Violence, 15*, 311-331.

Kocsis, R. N., & Palermo, G. B. (2007). Contemporary problems in criminal profiling. In R. N.

Kocsis (Ed.), *Criminal profiling: International theory, research, and practice* (pp. 327-345). Totowa, New Jersey: Humana Press.

Kuznetsov, A., Pierson, T. R., & Harry, B. (1992). Victim age as a basis for profiling sex offenders. *Federal Probation, 56*, 34–38.

Labuschange, G. (2006). The use of linkage analysis as evidence in the conviction of the Newcastle serial murderer, South Africa. *Journal of Investigative Psychology and Offender Profiling, 3*, 183-191.

Langer, W. (1972) *The Mind of Adolf Hitler. The Secret Wartime Report,* Basic Books, New York.

Laukkanen, M., & Santtila, P. (2005). Predicting the residential location of a serial commercial robber. *Forensic Science International,* 157, 71-82.

LeBeau, J. L. (1987a). The Journey to Rape: Geographic Distance and the Rapist's Method of Approaching the Victim. *Journal of Police Science and Administration*, 15, 129-136.

LeBeau, J. L. (1987b). The Methods and Measures of Centrography and the Spatial Dynamics of Rape. *Journal of Quantitative Criminology*, 3, 125-141.

LeBeau, J. L. (1987c). Patterns of Stranger and Serial Rape Offending: Factors Distinguishing Apprehended and at Large Offenders. *The Journal of Criminal Law & Criminology,* 78 (2), 309-326.

Lundrigan, S., & Canter, D. (2001a). A Multivariate Analysis of Serial Murderers' Disposal Site Location Choice. *Journal of Environmental Psychology*, 21, 423-432.

Lundrigan, S., & Canter, D. (2001b). Research Report: Spatial Patterns of Serial Murder: An Analysis of Disposal Site Location Choice. *Behavioural Sciences and the Law*, 19, 595-610.

Lucy, J. (1995) Offender profiling: what is it and what does it have to offer? unpublished paper, School of Law, Flinders University.

Lynch, I. & Dale, A. (1994) Profiling the burglars, *Police Review*, 102, 18-19.

Malocco, D.E. (2014) *Serial Sex Killers: Real American Killers,* Amazon

Malocco, D.E (2014) *Forensic Science: Crime Scene Analysis*, Amazon

Markson, L., Woodhams, J., & Bond, J.W. (2010). Linking serial residential burglary: comparing the utility of modus operandi behaviours, geographical proximity, and temporal proximity. *Journal of Investigative Psychology and Offender Profiling, 7*, 91-107.

McCann, J.T. (1992) Criminal personality profiling in the investigation of violent crime: recent advances and future directions, *Behavioral Sciences and the Law*, 10, 475-81.

Meaney, R. (2004). Commuters and Marauders: An Examination of the Spatial Behaviour of Serial Criminals. Journal of Investigative Psychology and Offender Profiling, 1 (2), 121-137.

Megargee, E.I. (1982) Psychological determinants and correlates of criminal violence, in *Criminal Violence*, eds M,E. Wolfgang & N.A. Weiner, Sage, Beverly Hills.

Mischel, W., Shoda, Y., & Mendoza-Denton, R. (2002). Situation-behavior profiles as a locus of consistency in personality. *Current Directions in Psychological Science, 11*, 50-54.

Mokros, A., & Alison, L. J. (2002). Is offender profiling possible? Testing the predicted homology of crime scene actions and background characteristics in a sample of rapists. *Legal and Criminological Psychology*, *7*, 25-43.

Morley, M. & Clark, S. (1993) *Murder in Mind*, Boxtree, London.

Morrison, R. (I995) Profiling aberrant sexual behavior: abnormal patterns can predict future crimes, *Law and Order*, 43(3), I00-102.

Murphy, W.D. & Peters, J.M. (1992) Profiling child sexual abusers: psychological considerations', *Criminal Justice and Behavior*, 19 ( 1 ), 24-37.

Muller, D. A. (2000). Criminal profiling: Real science or just wishful thinking? *Homicide Studies, 4*, 234-264.

Myers, W.C., Husted, D.S., Safarik, M.E., & O'Toole, M.E. (2006). The motivation behind serial sexual homicide: Is it sex, power, and control, or anger? *Journal of Forensic Sciences*, 51, 900-907.

Nowikowski, F. (1995) Psychological offender profiling: an overview, *The Criminologist*, 19(4), 255-73.

Nichols, W. W. Jr. (1980). Mental maps, social characteristics and criminal mobility. In D. E. Georges-Abeyie & K. D. Harries, (Eds.), *Crime: A Spatial Perspective* (pp.156-166). Columbia University Press.

Oldfield, D. (1997). What help do the police need with their enquiries? In J.L. Jackson & D.A. Berekian (Eds.), Offender profiling: Theory, research and practice (pp. 93-106). Chichester, England: Wiley.

Palermo, G.B, & Kocsis, R.N. (2005). *Offender profiling: An introduction to the sociopsychological analysis of violent crime.* Springfield, Ill: Charles C. Thomas Publisher Ltd.

Paulsen, D.J. (2006). Connecting the dots: Assessing the accuracy of geographic profiling software. Policing: *An International Journal of Police Strategies and Management*, 29(2), 306-334.

Paulsen, D. J. (2006). Human versus machine: A comparison of the accuracy of geographic profiling methods. *Journal of Investigative Psychology and Offender Profiling*, 3, 77-89.

Paulsen, D.J. (2007). Improving Geographic Profiling through Commuter/ Marauder Prediction.

Pettiway, L. E. (1982). Mobility of Burglars and Robbery Offenders. *Urban Affairs Quarterly*, 18(2), 255-270.

Phillips, P. D. (1980). Characteristics and typology of the journey to crime. In D. E. Georges-Abeyie & K. D. Harries, (Eds.), *Crime: A Spatial Perspective.* Columbia University Press.

Pinizzotto, A. J. (1984). Forensic psychology: Criminal personality profiling. *Journal of Police Science & Administration*, 12, 32-40.

Pinizzotto, A. J., & Finkel, N. J. (1990). Criminal personality profiling: An outcome and process study. *Law and Human Behavior*, 14, 215-233.

Pinto, S. & Wilson, P. (1992) Serial murder, in *Issues in Crime, Morality and Justice,* ed P. Wilson, Australian Institute of Criminology, Canberra, 157-73.

Proulx, J., & Beauregard, E. (2002). Profiles of the offending process of nonserial sexual murderers. *International Journal of Offender Therapy and Comparative Criminology*, 46, 386-399.

Proulx, J., Perreault, C., & Ouimet, M. (1999). Pathways in the offending process of extrafamilial sexual child molesters. *Sexual Abuse: A Journal of Research and Treatment*, 11, 117-129.

Ragg, M. (1992) Killers beware, *The Bulletin*, 11, 2.

Rayment, M. (1995) Inside the mind of a criminal, *NSW Police News*, 75, 15-18.

Reiser, M. (1982). Police psychology: Collected papers. Los Angeles: LEHI Publishing Company Royal Canadian Mounted Police. (n.d.). RCMP Violent Crime Linkage System (ViCLAS).

Rengert, G. F., Piquero, A. R., & Jones, P. R. (1999). Distance Decay Re-Examined. *Criminology*, 37 (2), 427-425.

Ressler, R., Burgess, A., & Douglas, J. (1988). *Sexual homicide: Patterns and motives.* New York: The Free Press.

Ressler, R.K., & Douglas, J.E. (1985). Crime scene and profile characteristics of organized and disorganized murderers. *FBI Law Enforcement Bulletin,* 58, 18-25.

Ressler, R.K., Burgess, A.W., Depue, R.L., Douglas, J.E. & Hazelwood, R.R. (1985) Classifying sexual homicide crime scenes, *FBI Law Enforcement Bulletin,* 54(8), 12-18.

Ressler, R.K., Burgess, A.W., Depue, R.L., Douglas, J.E. & Hazelwood, R.R. (1985) Crime scene and profile characteristics of organised and disorganised murderers, *FBI Law Enforcement Bulletin,* 54(8), 18-26.

Ressler, R.K., Burgess, A.W., Douglas, J.E., Hartman, C.R. & D'Agnostino, R.B. (1986) Sexual killers and their victims: identifying patterns through crime scene analysis, *Journal of Interpersonal Violence,* 1,288-308.

Ressler, R.K., Douglas, J.E., Burgess, A.W. & Burgess, A.G. (1992) *Crime Classification Manual,* Simon & Schuster, London.

Ressler, R.K., Douglas, J.E., Groth, A.N. & Burgess, A.W. (1980) Offender profiles: a multidisciplinary approach, *FBI Law Enforcement Bulletin,* 49(9), 16-20.

Ressler, R.K. & Schactman, R. (1992) *Whoever Fights Monsters,* Simon & Schuster, London.

Rhodes, W. M., & Conly, C. (1981). Crime and Mobility: An Empirical Study. In P. J. Brantingham, & P. L. Brantingham (Eds.), *Environmental Criminology* (pp. 167-188). Beverley Hills: Sage Publications.

Rider, A.O. (1980) The firesetter: a psychological profile, part II', *FBI Law Enforcement Bulletin*, 49(7), 7-17.

Robertiello, G., & Terry, K.J. (2007). Can we profile sex offenders? A review of sex offenders typologies. *Aggression and Violent Behaviour*, 12, 508-518.

Rossi, D. (1982), 'Crime Scene Behavioural Analysis: Another Tool for the Law Enforcement Investigator', Official proceedings of the 88th Annual IACP Conference, *The Police Chief*, January, pp. 156-59.

Rossmo, D. K. (1995). Place, space, and police investigations: Hunting serial violent criminals. In J. E. Eck & D. L. Weisburd (Eds.), *Crime and place: Crime prevention studies*, Vol. 4 (pp. 217-235). Monsey, NY: Criminal Justice Press.

Rossmo, K. (1997). Geographic Profiling. In J. L. Jackson and D. A. Bekerian (Eds.), *Offender Profiling: Theory, Research and Practice,* (pp 159-176). New York: John Wiley and Sons.

Rossmo, K. (2005). Geographic Heuristics or Shortcuts to Failure?: Response to Snook et al. *Applied Cognitive Psychology,* 19 (5), 531-678.

Rumbelow, D. (1988) *The Complete Jack the Ripper*, Penguin, London.

Salfati, G.C., & Bateman, A.L. (2005). Serial homicide: An investigation of behavioural consistency. *Journal of Investigative Psychology and Offender Profiling*, 2, 121-144.

Salfati, G., & Taylor, P. (2006). Differentiating sexual violence: A comparison of sexual homicide and rape. *Psychology, Crime and Law*, 12, 107-125.

Santtila, P., Fritzon, K., & Tamelander, A. L. (2005). Linking arson incidents on the basis of crime scene behavior. *Journal of Police and Criminal Psychology*, 19, 1–16.

Santtila, P., Hakkanen, H., Canter, D., & Elfgren, T. (2003). Classifying homicide offenders and predicting their characteristics from crime scene behaviour. *Scandinavian Journal of Psychology*, 44, 107-118.

Santtila, P., Pakkanen, T., Zappala, A., Bosco, D., Valkama, M., & Mokros, A. (2008). Behavioural crime linking in serial homicide. *Psychology, Crime and Law,* 14, 245- 265.

Santtila, P., Korpela, S., & Hakkanen, H. (2004). Expertise and Decision Making in the Linking of Car Crime Series. *Psychology, Crime & Law*, 10(2), 97-112.

Santtila, P., Zappala, A., Laukkanen, M., & Picozzi, M. (2003). Testing the utility of a geographical profiling approach in three rape series of a single offender: A case study. *Forensic Science International*, 131, 42-52.

Sarangi, S. & Youngs, D. (2006). Spatial patterns of Indian serial burglars with relevance to geographical profiling. . *Journal of Investigative Psychology and Offender Profiling*, 3, 105-115.

Sarangi, S., & Youngs, D. (2006). Spatial Patterns of Indian Serial Burglars with Relevance to Geographical Profiling. *Journal of Investigative Psychology and Offender Profiling*, 3, 105-115.

Saucier, G., & Goldberg, L.R. (1996). Evidence for the Big Five in analyses of familiar English personality adjectives. *European Journal of Personality,* 10, 61-77.

Siegal, L and C. McCormick. (2006). *Criminology in Canada: Theories, Patterns, and Typologies* (3rd ed.). Toronto: Thompson, Nelson

Simpson, L. & Harvey, S. (1994) *The Killer Next Door: Death in an Australian Suburb*, Random House, Sydney.

Slahor, S. (1991) Making profiling work, *Law and Order*, 39(4), 76-77.

Smith, C. (1993) Psychological offender profiling, *The Criminologist*, 17(4), 244-45.

Snook, B., Cullen, R.M., Bennell, C., Taylor, P.J., & Gendreau, P. (2008). The criminal profiling illusion: What's behind the smoke and mirrors? *Criminal Justice and Behavior,* 35, 1257-1276.

Snook, B., Eastwood, J., Gendreau, P., Goggin, C., & Cullen, R. M. (2007). Taking stock of criminal profiling: A narrative review and meta-analysis. *Criminal Justice and Behavior*, 34, 437-453.

Snook, B., Luther, K., House, J.C., Bennell, C., & Taylor, P. (2012). The Violent Crime Linkage Analysis System: A test of interrater reliability. *Criminal Justice and Behavior*, 39, 607-619.

Snook, B., Cullen, R. M., Mokros, A., & Harbort, S. (2005). Serial Murderers' Spatial Decisions: Factors That Influence Crime Location Choice. *Journal of Investigative Psychology and Offender Profiling*, 2(3), pp 147-164.

Snook, B., Wright, M. House, J. C., Alison, L. J. (2006). Searching for a needle in a needle stack: Combining criminal careers and journey-to-crime research for criminal suspect prioritization. *Police Practice and Research*, 7(3), 217-230.

Snook, B., Zito, M., Bennell, C., & Taylor, P. J. (2005). On the complexity and accuracy of geographic profiling strategies. *Journal of Quantitative Criminology*, 21(1), 1-26.

Snook, B. (2004). Individual Differences in Distances Travelled by Serial Burglars. *Journal of Investigative Psychology and Offender Profiling*, 1 (1), 53-66.

Snook, B., Canter, D., & Bennell, C. (2002). Predicting the Home Location of Serial Offenders: A Preliminary Comparison of the Accuracy of Human Judges with a Geographic Profiling System. *Behavioral Sciences and the Law*, 20, 109-118.

Tamura, M., & Suzuki, M. (2000). Characteristics of Serial Arsonists and Crime Scene Geography in Japan.

Ter Beek, M., Van Den Eshof, P., & Mali, B. (2010). Statistical modelling in the investigation of stranger rape. *Journal of Investigative Psychology and Offender Profiling*, 7, 31-47.

Tonkin, M., Bond, J.W., & Woodhams, J. (2009). Fashion conscious burglars? Testing the principles of offender profiling with footwear impressions recovered at domestic burglaries. *Psychology, Crime & Law*, 15, 327-345.

Tuchman, B. (1967) Can history use Freud? The case of Woodrow Wilson, *The Atlantic Monthly*, 3, 39-44.

Turco, R. (1990). Psychological profiling. *International Journal of Offender Therapy and Comparative Criminology*, 34, 147-154.

Vandiver, J. (1982) Crime profiling shows promise, *Law and Order*, 30(10), 33-78.

Van Koppen, P. J., & De Keiser, J. W. (1997). Desisting Distance Decay: On the Aggregation of Individual Crime Trips. *Criminology*, 35 (2), 505-513.

Van Koppen, P. J., & Jansen, R. W. (1998). The Road to Robbery: Travel Patterns in Commercial Robberies. British *Journal of Criminology*, 38 (2), 230-246.

Van Zandt, C.R. & Ether, S.E. (1994) The real Silence of the Lambs', *Police Chief* 11(4), 45-52.

Vorpogel, R.E. (1982), Painting Psychological Profiles, Charlatism, Charisma, or a New Science?, *The Police Chief*, January, pp. 156-9.

Walker, J., Golden, J., & Van Houten, A. (2001). The Geographic Link Between Sex Offenders and Potential Victims: A Routine Activities Approach. *Justice Research Policy*, 3(2), 15-33.

Walter, R. (1987) Sex killers: their actions and reactions, *Australian Police Journal*, 92-97.

Warren, J., Reboussin, R., Hazelwood, R. R., Cummings, A., Gibbs, N., & Trumbetta, S. (1998). Crime Scene and Distance Correlates of Serial Rape. *Journal of Quantitative Criminology*, 14 (1), 35-59.

Warren, J.I., Hazelwood, R.R., &Dietz, P.E. (1996). The sexually sadistic serial killer. *Journal of Forensic Sciences*, 41, 970-974.

Warren, J., Reboussin, R., Hazelwood, R., Gibbs, N., Trumbetta, S., & Cummings, A. (1999). Crime scene analysis and the escalation of violence in serial rape. *Forensic Science International*, 100, 37-56.

Warren, J., Reboussin, R., Hazelwood, R.R., Cummings, A., Gibbs, N., & Trumbetta, S. (1998). Crime scene and distance correlates of serial rape. *Journal of Quantitative Criminology*, 14, 35-59.

Weiner, M.D., Sussman, S., Sun, P., & Dent, C. (2005). Explaining the link between violence perpetration, victimization and drug use. *Addictive Behaviors*, 30, 1261-1266.

White, R. C. (1932). The Relation of Felonies to Environmental Factors in Indianapolis. *Social Forces* 10(4), 498-509.

Wiles, P., & Costello, A. (2000). The "road to nowhere": The evidence for travelling criminals. *Home Office research study* 207

Wilson, A., & Alison, L. (2004). Questioning sequences in Canadian police interviews: Constructing and confirming the course of events? *Psychology, Crime and Law*, 10, 137-154.

Wilson, C. & Seaman, D. (1992) *The Serial Killers*, Cox and Wyman, London.

Wilson, P. (1986) Serial and lust murder: questions on police management and response, *Australian Police Journal,* November, 2-8.

Wilson, P. (1990) Sex and crime, *Australian Journal of Forensic Sciences,* 22(3), 93-100.

# ABOUT THE AUTHOR

David Elio Malocco was born in Dundalk, County Louth, Ireland. His father was born in Casalattico in Frosinone in Italy and his mother was born in Monaghan in Ireland. He was educated at the Christian Brothers School in Dundalk and his parents later sent him to St. Patrick's College in Cavan where they hoped he would be ordained as a Roman Catholic priest. But he chose law and business instead.

He received his Bachelor of Civil Law degree from University College Dublin and spent fifteen years as a criminal lawyer before taking a second degree at the Open University, Milton Keynes in England where he obtained a first class honors degree in Psychology majoring in Cognitive Development.

In 1991 he realized a personal ambition and moved to New York where he studied film direction, production and writing for film at New York University. Since then he has written numerous screenplays in several genre and has written, produced and directed several shorts and three feature films, *Virgin Cowboys, Magdalen* and *Jack Gambel: The Enigma.*

He later studied creative writing at Oxford University and since then has completed a Higher Certificate in Psychotherapy; a Professional Certificate in Stockbroking from the Institute of Banking and is currently completing a Masters in Financial Services from University College Dublin..

He is a graduate member of the British Psychological Society; and a member of the Association of Professional Counsellors and Psychotherapists; the American Criminology Society; and, the Institute of Banking.

He has written several books on true crime and forensic science. The books were motivated by dual diplomas he had taken. The first was in the Psychology of Criminal Profiling and the second in Forensic Science specializing in crime scene analysis. But his repertoire of writing also includes comedy, cooking, conspiracy theories and health books.

His publications include:

*A Brief History of Criminal Profiling*
*A Brief History of Psychology*
*Approaches in Criminal Profiling*

*The Beatles Conspiracy: John, Paul, George, Ringo and Bill*
*Criminal Profiling*
*Eat Yourself Thin Fat Bitch*
*How to Commit the Perfect Murder: Forensic Science Analyzed*
*I am a Cannibal: A Study of Anthropophagy;*
*Murder for Profit: They Killed for Money;*
*Psychotherapy: The Top 50 Theorists and Theories*
*Psychotherapy: Approaches and Theories*
*Serial Sex Killers: Real American Psychos;*
*Sexual Psychopaths: British Serial Killers;*
*The Beatles Conspiracy: John, Paul, George, Ringo and Bill!;*
*Whacker Hennessy's Fifty Alcohol Infused Classic Recipes*
*Which Therapy?*
*Who's Who Serial Killers: The Top 100;*
*Wicked Women;*
*The World's Worst Serial Killers;*

David is a lifelong supporter of Liverpool Football Club and enjoys filmmaking, writing, drinking wine, cooking and rescuing abandoned and abused dogs.

You can email him on davidmalocco@gmail.com

CPSIA information can be obtained
at www.ICGtesting.com
Printed in the USA
LVHW040906180723
752741LV00004B/500